BUILDING & MAINTAINING A CHURCH STAFF

Building & Maintaining a Church Staff

Leonard E. Wedel

BROADMAN PRESS
Nashville, Tennessee

4225-09
ISBN: 0-8054-2509-8

Dewey Decimal Classification Number: 254
Library of Congress catalog card number: 67:12177
Printed in the United States of America

To Nita

Contents

[illegible]

Although [illegible] staffs [illegible] may vary in size, their purpose is to perform tasks that [illegible] sustain the four common functions of a church: to preach the gospel, to worship, to educate the members, and [illegible] ministries. The church's mission is the staff's mission. The church's goals are the staff's goals.

This concept places a grave responsibility on the pastor to lead

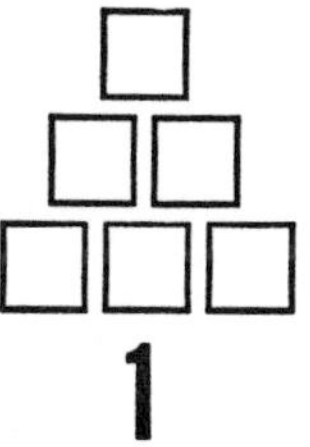

1

Getting the Right Person on the Right Job

A pastor needs all the help he can get.

So does the minister of education, minister of music, and the church business administrator.

As supervisors these people plan, organize, and coordinate the work of other paid staff members. They motivate and direct workers in the performance of their tasks, check their progress, and evaluate results. They try to coordinate the work of several people to accomplish more effectively the purposes of the church.

However, church staff supervisors cannot carry the full load of staff administration. They need help. The most logical source is the personnel committee. This committee is made up of lay people with the pastor as an ex officio member. Their responsibility is to work through the pastor in all matters related to paid staff personnel administration.

Although paid staffs of churches may vary in size, their purpose is to perform tasks that support and sustain the four common functions of a church: to preach the gospel; to worship; to educate the members; and to perform church ministries. The church's mission is the staff's mission. The church's goals are the staff's goals.

This concept places a grave responsibility on the pastor to lead staff workers to reach and maintain high levels of workmanship and interpersonnel relationships.

The pastor is not separate from the staff team but is a member of it. At times he gives leadership, guidance, and direction; at other times he follows the counsel and suggestions of other staff members. The blending of knowing how to lead and how to follow is basic to growing and developing a staff team.

Most pastors and other staff supervisors want to be a part of a well-managed staff. So do the secretaries, receptionists, clerks, and janitors.

Building and maintaining a well-managed staff begins by getting the right person for each job. The quality, dedication, and morale of the several members who comprise the paid staff contribute greatly to the overall attainment of a church's goals.

Quality shows in a number of ways—evidence of spiritual concern, genuine desire to serve, and job skills of staff workers. The pastor, minister of education, minister of music, and others are measured by their ability to lead the people to plan, organize, and execute church programs of work.

Quality shows in other ways. Letters neatly typed and framed on the page speak well of a church. Attractive church bulletins, either printed or duplicated by office machines, create favorable and positive attitudes of members toward the church's total program. Accurate office financial and educational records provide incentives to volunteer workers who have Sunday record-keeping duties. The receptionist creates goodwill for the church when she receives visitors, members, and vendors cordially and helpfully.

Goodwill is also created when staff workers follow through on promises they make to church members. An entire staff is sometimes affected adversely when one paid worker is careless about following through on commitments. For example, one church had a paid worker who usually said, "Yes, I'll do that," but seldom did. Church leaders were confused and frustrated when they found the kitchen unavailable after it had been promised for a certain time; or the room assigned was not cleaned and arranged; or the church doors were locked when a meeting had been scheduled; or educational supplies were not purchased; or needed workers had not been enlisted.

All in all, the paid staff can affect the general attitude and optimisim of the entire church. The church, then, has a vital interest in the quality and dedication of its staff workers. The pastor and other staff supervisors have the responsibility of obtaining the best possible workers.

The story is told of an employee who was suddenly promoted. Every good thing began to come his way. One of his friends could not understand his miraculous rise and asked him how it happened.

"Well," he began obviously puzzled, "the only way I can figure it out is that one day I wore my golf shoes to work and accidently stepped on my IBM card."

Getting the right person on the right job is not so easily accomplished.

The overall selection process may involve several personal interviews with one or more applicants, the giving of typing, shorthand, and other tests, the following up of business and character references, and the evaluation of all the accumulated information before the final decision is reached to employ or not to employ a certain person.

Some supervisors chafe under what they describe as a tedious selection process. They devise short cuts. After sizing up a person only a few minutes, they feel infallibly guided by some intuitive sense—"She is what we're looking for," or, "She isn't."

Both men and women are afflicted with this snap judgment disease. The best cure is to keep in mind some of the deplorable mistakes made along the way. Some persons who were expected to succeed failed; others who were expected to fail succeeded—somewhere else!

Even after a thorough checking of an applicant's qualifications, one may vacillate between two choices: to employ or not to employ. The reference follow-ups, test scores, and interviews affirm the applicant's potential. Still one hesitates until the pressures of mounting work push him to a decision.

The dilemma may be compared to the middle-aged couple who asked the banker for a loan. He was dubious. However, the wife supported her husband's request so convincingly the banker agreed. After the husband signed the note and got the money she turned to the banker and said, "You're a lousy judge of character."

Sometimes employment decisions prove to be misjudgments. However, in spite of the varying degrees of confidence or anxiety about making a decision, it must be done.

These suggestions may be helpful in employing the right person for the job.

Establish Job Qualifications

Suppose there is a clerical vacancy in the church office. What kind of a person should be sought? To what extent would such things as age, clerical skills, experience, education enter into the consideration? Job qualifications serve as guidelines to help in the selection of the most qualified person for the job.

In many churches vacancies occur infrequently. Nevertheless, a list of job qualifications is important. Even one termination in several years makes a set of qualifications a welcome support.

The following questions may prompt suggestions that will help in setting up a church's employment qualifications.

- What are the minimum and maximum age limits under and over which the church will not employ?
- What are the minimum educational requirements for the various jobs on the staff?
- Is a worker required to be a member of the church, another church of like denomination, or does church membership make any difference?
- What minimum typing speed is required for each clerical job?
- What minimum shorthand speed is required for the jobs of stenographer or secretary?
- Would more than one person from the same household be employed?

- Is previous job experience required?
- What health requirements, if any, should be established?

Several advantages are provided by church-approved job qualifications: (1) the preliminary interview can be performed more quickly; (2) an applicant can be dealt with more straightforwardly and encouraged or discouraged in further pursuit of a job in the church; and (3) refusal to a church member, parent, or a prominent church leader who wishes employment of a person obviously not qualified for the job is supported.

A church policy covering job qualifications loses its effectiveness when exceptions are made. For example, a supervisor in one church employed an office worker whose membership was elsewhere—an exception to the policy. A year later he interviewed a person for another office job vacancy. He explained that if the applicant were employed, she would be required to join the local church. She replied, "Why should I? You have a person on your staff who is a member of another church." It is doubtful the supervisor presented a convincing rebuttal.

Another staff supervisor learned about exceptions the hard way. The applicant seated before him met all job requirements except typing speed. She typed approximately 30 words a minute which was less than required for the job. After explaining the required skill for the job to the applicant, she pleaded, "If you'll only give me a chance, I'll increase my speed on the job." With the understanding that she would improve her typing skill, the supervisor agreed to employ her. Six months later very little improvement was evident.

In the meantime, the other clerical workers in the office were patient and helped the new girl get started. However, they soon became aware that her lack of typing skill affected adversely several areas of work flow. They wondered why the supervisor would employ a person who couldn't "cut the mustard"—and who could blame them!

On the other hand, it is possible to establish minimum job qualifications so high and rigid that finding replacements becomes difficult. For example, to require a college degree, or even one or two years of college, for a clerical job may narrow considerably the field of applicants.

Establishing job qualifications is a significant part of overall management in a church office. The pastor and the personnel committee should take the initiative in setting up employment qualifications.

It is important that every supervisor on the church staff follow whatever qualification guidelines are established. The paid staff creates serious problems for itself when each supervisor—pastor, minister of education, minister of music, church business administrator—has his own set of job qualifications.

Prepare an Application Form

The application form includes a variety of questions designed to get factual information about an applicant. The application form is a useful tool to help the supervisor reach a decision to employ the right person.

In preparing a job application form, decide what basic information is wanted about each applicant. Generally, application blanks include questions covering personal data, education, employment history, skills, ability, experience, health, and references. You may wish to include a section on church affiliation and activity. See Exhibit I for a sample job application form.

Although few persons may ask about a job in the church, still an application form is well worth having. Ask each applicant to complete this form. When there is a vacancy, the completed applications on file will serve as ready references. After one or two years, applications are of little value, so update the files annually. Write the applicants and request them to indicate their continued interest on an enclosed, self-addressed card.

Explore Applicant Possibilities

How does one go about finding a qualified replacement when a vacancy occurs or a qualified worker when expansion becomes necessary? One supervisor said, "First, if the person who left us was 'tops,' I'd go somewhere and cry."

EXHIBIT I

APPLICATION FORM (Sample)

______________________________Church

Date______________________________

I. PERSONAL DATA

Name (last)______________(first)_____________(middle)______________
Address(street)____
(city)___________________(state)_____________(zip code)____________
Phone Number________________(Social Security Number)______________
Birth Date (month)_______________(day)______________(year)___________
Marital Status: Single___Married___Divorced___Separated___Widow___

II. EDUCATION

High School Diploma: yes____ no____; if yes, when?________________
Business College: yes____no____; if yes, where located?____________
University or College: yes___no___; if yes, did you graduate?____
What was your major?__________________Minor?_____________________
Name and location of college______________________________________
Seminary: yes____no____; if yes, did you graduate?________________
Degree_____________Where is Seminary located?____________________
School or college activities in which you engaged?__________________
____

III. EMPLOYMENT HISTORY (Start with present or most recent job)

1. Name of Employer____
Address____
Worked from_____to_____Monthly salary or hourly rate__________
Type of work performed____
Reason for leaving____

2. Name of Employer____
Address____
Worked from______to______Monthly salary or hourly rate________
Reason for leaving____

3. Name of Employer____
Address____
Worked from______to______Monthly salary or hourly rate__________
Reason for leaving____

(Please complete reverse side)

EXHIBIT I

APPLICATION FORM (Sample)
(Page 2)

IV. JOB DATA (Check areas in which you have had experience or training)

____Typing (Speed____WPM)
____Shorthand (Speed____WPM)
____Transcribing Machine
____Bookkeeping
____Duplicating Machine
____Addressograph Machine

____Receptionist
____Writing and Editing
____Supervisor
____Custodian
____
____

V. CHURCH LIFE

Denomination____
Name of Church (Where you hold membership)________________
Location____
What church activities did (do) you participate in?__________
____

VI. HEALTH

How would you describe your general health?______________
Hearing?____________________Eyesight?__________________
Physical defects, if any?__________________________
Date of last physical examination____________________

VII. CHARACTER REFERENCES (Do not list relatives or former employers)

1. Name____________________Address____________________
   Occupation________________Years Known________________

2. Name____________________Address____________________
   Occupation________________Years Known________________

3. Name____________________Address____________________
   Occupation________________Years Known________________

VIII. ADDITIONAL INFORMATION

Please give us any additional information you desire about your education and experience (Include any special talents)

Please Sign Your Name________________________________

Although this feeling of regret is normal, the supervisor must give immediate attention to finding a qualified replacement.

Some supervisors fall into self-devised traps by insisting on "finding another person just like Louise." This is wishful thinking.

What he may mean is that now he has to assume some of his own tasks that he had assigned to Louise. Or he will miss all the extra things Louise did for him and his wife, such as deposit his check, make personal purchases, pay his bills, baby-sit at his home occasionally, and sometimes buy his family's weekly supply of groceries. Or Louise was the only one in the office who always agreed with him on any idea he proposed. Or Louise was an excellent worker and a good team member.

A sobering thought to consider about replacement is: Suppose someone or some committee of a church looked for a person exactly like some predecessor. If a successor is selected on that basis, how can he possibly perform as two people? And yet, somehow, a "Louise wall" is unintentionally built when a replacement is being sought. The opposite opinion, "We don't want another Louise, that's for sure," may be just as bad. How then should replacements be secured?

A sensible and positive approach is to consider the church's interest, to find a person who best fits the job requirements. Believe it or not, a new worker may have some traits and abilities superior to any former worker.

First, restudy the job requirements. This is a good rule to follow after each termination. Plan a conference with the worker a week or so before termination. Go over every aspect of the job —what is done regularly, occasionally, and infrequently. Later, as notes about the job are studied, needed changes in work assignments affecting the work of other persons in the office may be discovered. Review the suggested changes with the other employees and ask for their comments and ideas. One may or may not wish to incorporate all of their suggestions in the revised job description.

Second, check to see if the vacancy is a promotion possibility for a worker in the office. If so, promote the person then seek a replacement for the new vacancy.

Third, check the application file for prospects. If none qualifies, look through the names on the church roll, unless, of course, job qualifications preclude their consideration.

The placement bureau in one's town or city may provide some leads. The local business college is another recruiting source. For some church jobs, high school graduates with or without business experience are another source. Sometimes the businessmen in the church membership are able and willing to give helpful information. A pastor or minister of education of another church may be able to furnish the name of a prospective applicant.

When talking to others about the vacancy, be sure to describe briefly the job duties and qualifications. To say that a secretary's job is open in the church is misleading. The word *secretary* means different things to different people. For some, it means the highest paid office job in the church. For others, it may mean the person who keeps the records.

Sometimes an applicant learns of the vacancy through friends, neighbors, the paid staff workers, or church members. The applicant may call by telephone to ask for more job information. If he is interested invite him to the office for further talk.

When a job is vacant for a few weeks, some supervisors get panicky and in desperation employ a person who does not meet the job requirements. The better practice is to employ a temporary worker during the interim period, or to get volunteer office help from church members.

Interview the Applicant

The interview can be a pleasant and profitable experience or it can be dull and drab. How the interview moves depends largely on the ability of the interviewer. The following suggestions may be helpful.

- Arrange an appointment. Schedule a time which is mutually convenient. If the applicant is already employed, schedule the interview during his free time.

Some applicants do not make an appointment. They walk in and expect someone to talk to them. Do so, if at all possible.

• Plan for the interview. Tell the receptionist or secretary that an applicant (give name) is expected at a certain time. Request that the person be assisted to fill in the application form. When it is completed, the form should be taken to the interviewer while the applicant waits in the outer office. Before the applicant is received the interviewer should do two things: review the job duties and skill qualifications of the position in question and check the completed application form. Ask the secretary to take telephone calls during the interview.

Another important item in preparation is to tidy up the desk. A cluttered desk, or one piled high with papers—even though in neat stacks, may make the applicant feel that he is intruding on one's worktime. Also, if one knows himself to be a "pencil-on-desk-tapper," he should place pencils and pens out of reach.

• Keep the appointment. Not only keep the appointment, but be on time! An appointment is akin to a personal pledge—a promise.

If it is impossible to be present at the specified time, ask the secretary to tell the person waiting about the delay and of the expected time of return.

Or, if one is in his office but tied up on a project which must be finished in ten or fifteen minutes, ask the secretary to explain the brief delay. Or, better yet, walk out of the office for a moment to meet the person, apologize for the delay and tell him that the interview will take place in just a few moments.

• Greet the applicant warmly. Make him feel welcome. Open the interview by conversing briefly and informally about some subject of mutual interest. Information on the application form usually provides good leads. Not many applicants are "old hands" at job interviewing. They are nervous, sit stiffly, and are usually somewhat frightened. Cordial greetings and opening remarks can do much to relax both participants in the interview.

• Talk face to face. Face-to-face dialogue is the best way for people to know each other. Keep in mind that the purpose of the interview is to discover the applicant's qualifications. Employ no trick questions during the interview. Do not try to angle the applicant into a trap. Do not intentionally confuse or embarrass the applicant. Being anything less than one's best self is a reflection on the integrity of the church represented.

• Do little of the talking. Talk only enough to keep the conversation informal and friendly. Avoid expressing opinions or telling personal experiences.

Some interviews are a disappointment to the applicant because the interviewer talks mainly about his job, or family, or the hard time he had getting an education, or about his hobbies. Seemingly, every contribution the applicant makes to the interview prompts a recall of the interviewer's experiences.

A good interviewer encourages the applicant to talk. He asks questions that call for narrative statements rather than for an expression of opinions. For example, he may ask: Tell me about your home and your parents. Tell me about your high school days, your teachers, subjects, activities. What do you do in your church? What are your future plans?

A good interviewer avoids asking leading questions such as: You do want to work don't you? Do you think you would like to work in a church office? You did get along with your previous supervisor, didn't you?

• Give the applicant undivided attention. This is not always easy to do, especially when there are time or job pressures. The applicant quickly senses any disinterest when one shuffles papers, or writes himself a note, or answers the telephone, or fidgets with pen, pencil, or some desk gadget.

The best way to give attention is to listen to what he says. Then follow-up questions are more pertinent. Also, one is more alert to what is not said.

• Answer questions. Before the interview is terminated, ask the applicant if he has any questions. It is important to observe the kind of questions asked. They can say a great deal about a person. However, do not automatically "blackball" a person because he asks poor or wrong questions.

• Conclude the interview courteously. Express appreciation to the person for interest in a job in the church.

Tell the applicant whether he does or does not qualify for the job. Generally, people appreciate the facts. Do not give employment hope to a person who does not qualify by concluding the interview with a remark such as, "We'll call you if we need to talk with you further."

Some supervisors try to ease the applicant's disappointment by talking in platitudes for several minutes. Meanwhile, the applicant knows by the tone of his voice and weak closing statements what he is trying to say. Most people prefer that the interviewer omit the wasted words and get to the point.

Getting to the point does not mean that one abruptly says, "You just don't qualify for the job." Rather, it means reaching a conclusion in the same warm and friendly spirit which pervaded the entire interview.

On the other hand, give the applicant encouragement if he seems to qualify for the job vacancy. Tell him that a follow-up will be made on previous work record and references before the next interview. Discuss briefly the salary of the job if the applicant is a good prospect. Salary is usually an unspoken question in the mind of the applicant. Salary information will help him decide the extent of his interest in the job which may later be offered.

Ask the applicant to take a typing speed test before leaving (or whatever tests the job requires). Suggestions on administering tests are given later in this chapter. There may or may not be time to score the tests before he leaves.

• Evaluate the interview. Record impressions immediately after the person leaves. The interviewer should ask himself these questions:

Who did most of the talking?

Did I cut off some of his comments by breaking into his remarks?

How much more do I know about the applicant than appears on the application form?

Did I express opinions?

How much of my negative impression is based on personal prejudice?

Am I giving proper weight, and no more, to personal appearance?

Was the interview more mechanical than personal?

What seem to be some of his positive and some of his negative qualities?

What are some of the things I would do differently if I had the opportunity to interview this applicant again?

• Check character and business references. The application form usually includes space for the applicant to name at least three people who have known him for several years and space for him to write in any prior work experience.

A follow-up on named references may be done either by writing or by telephoning for specific information about the applicant. Usually, more direct and accurate information can be obtained by telephoning. See Exhibit II for a suggested telephone reference follow-up form. If telephoning is impractical, write references for information. See Exhibit III for a sample form.

Written character references may not be too reliable. A person usually hesitates to write his candid opinion about an applicant who has named him as a character reference.

Business reference follow-ups usually give more specific and factual information. See Exhibit IV for a sample form.

Attach to the application form the reference follow-ups, test results, and the interview evaluation and impressions. This material serves as a ready reference for the second interview.

If the person proves to be a good possibility for employment, based upon the test results and follow-up references, do not wait too long before talking to him again. Qualified people do not look long for jobs.

• Conduct the second interview. The second interview, and perhaps a third in some cases, is arranged only if one is more

EXHIBIT II

TELEPHONE QUESTIONNAIRE

(Business Reference Guide)

Applicant's Name________________________Address____________________

Call made to______________________of____________________Phone______
(Company)

1. Verify dates of employment: From______________to______________

2. Was he under your supervision?_____If no, under whom?____________

3. What was his position in your firm?_____________________________

4. How would you rate his performance in that position?
   Above average____; Average____; Below average____

5. Why did he leave your employ?___________________________________

6. Could he have advanced if he had stayed with you?_______________
   If so, to what type of work?______________________________________

7. We are considering him for _______job. Do you think he can perform
   this type work?____________

8. How did he get along with his superiors? Well____Fairly well______
   Poorly_____

9. How did he get along with other workers? Well_____Fairly well_____
   Poorly_____

10. Was he dependable?_____

11. Was he regular in attendance and punctual?______________________

12. Would you rehire him if circumstances permitted?________________

13. To your knowledge does he have any undesirable habits?___________
    Speech____; Dress____; Personal hygiene____; Other____________

14. What are his strongest traits?__________________________________
    Weakest____

15. Is there any comment you would like to add which has not been
    discussed?____

16. Verify, if possible, the position and title of the person called

    ____

17. Person called was: Cooperative_________ Uncooperative__________
    Pleasant____________ Unpleasant_____________
    Knew facts__________ Hesitated______________
    Willing to help_____ Unwilling______________

Call made by_____________________Date______________________

EXHIBIT II

TELEPHONE QUESTIONNAIRE

(Character Reference Guide)

(Page 2)

Applicant's Name________________________ Address____________________

Call made to__________________________ Telephone_______________

Give some idea of the job for which applicant is being considered.

1. How long have you known the applicant?____________________

2. Are you a friend of the family?__________ A school friend__________
Through what source did you meet the applicant?__________

3. How does he spend his spare time? Sports?________ Reading?________
Hobby?________________________ Other?____________________

4. Does he have many or few friends?____________________

5 How does he get along with them?____________________

6. We understand he is a member of the________________________ Church
Does he attend regularly?______ What does he do in church work?
____

7. To your knowledge does he have any undesirable habits?__________
Speech_______; Dress_______; Personal hygiene_____; Other_____

8. What are his strongest traits?____________________
Weakest?____________________

9. Is there any comment you would like to add which has not been discussed?____________________

10. Person called was: Cooperative__________ Uncooperative__________
Pleasant__________ Unpleasant__________
Knew facts__________ Hesitated__________
Willing to help______ Unwilling__________

Call made by________________________ Date__________________

EXHIBIT III

CHARACTER REFERENCE INQUIRY

Please return to______________________________________Church

(Address) ____

(Person's name who will receive this information)______________

TO:____

ADDRESS:____DATE__________

NAME OF APPLICANT:_______________________________AGE__________

The applicant whose name appears above has made application with us for employment. Please give us information requested below and any additional comment. Information will be kept confidential.

1. How long have you known the applicant?____________________
2. Are you a friend of the family?_________________________
3. How does he spend his spare time?________________________
4. Where is his church membership?__________________________
5. Church attendance: regular___; irregular___; not at all________
6. Please rate the applicant

QUALIFICATIONS	EXCELLENT	GOOD	FAIR	POOR	DO NOT KNOW
Character					
Conduct					
Work attitude					
Ability to get along with others					
Cooperation					
Dependability					
Honesty					
Personal habits					
Emotional maturity					

7. Additional comments:

SIGNED____DATE__________

EXHIBIT IV

BUSINESS REFERENCE INQUIRY

Please return to______________________________Church

(Address)____

(Person's name who will receive this information)_______

TO:____

ADDRESS:_____________________________________DATE__________

NAME OF APPLICANT:____________________________AGE__________

The applicant whose name appears above has made application with us for employment. Please give us the information requested below and any additional comments. Information will be kept confidential.

1. Claims employment with you as______________yes___no_______
2. Worked with you from________to________yes___no___________
3. Was actually employed as ______________________________
4. At a beginning salary of___________closing salary of _______
5. Was laid off_____discharged_____left voluntarily__________
6. Would you reemploy? yes_____no_____If not, please give reasons ____
7. Please rate the applicant

QUALIFICATIONS	EXCELLENT	GOOD	FAIR	POOR	DO NOT KNOW
Character					
Job competence					
Loyalty					
Ability to get along with others					
Emotional maturity					
Personal habits					
Record of attendance and punctuality					

8. Additional comments:

SIGNED_______________________________DATE____________

POSITION____

than casually impressed with the applicant's potential. The purpose of this interview is to:

Review the applicant's file

Ask questions gleaned from reference follow-ups. (Do not reveal to the applicant the reference follow-up statements. This is confidential information.)

Review salary information

Discuss employee benefits

Offer him the job

Set a date for the applicant to report for work

Test for Job Skills

Results of typing, shorthand, and other clerical tests provide additional information for help in determining the employability of an applicant. Tests cannot measure what a person *will* do on the job; only what he *can* do. An indiscriminate use of tests is not recommended.

Most churches do not have staff members who are schooled in the use of tests. Some churches, however, are located in cities that have a state employment office. This office will serve without charge. Make the acquaintance of an official and learn of these services. When an applicant is employable, refer him to the employment office for typing and other tests.

If a church is located in a city or town which does not have these testing services, typing and shorthand tests can be given in the church office.

For typing speed tests, use material from a typing manual or prepare copy. Copy consists of accurately pretyped material of moderate word difficulty. In the white space on the right-hand margin of the copy write in the running total of the number of strokes in each line of type. Add the total of each line to the one following. For example, the first line may have 62 strokes counting characters and punctuation (but not spaces between words). The total number of strokes in the second line may be 64, making the figure in the margin to the right of the second line 126 (62 plus 64). Continue figuring the running line total. The figure in the right-hand margin of the last line may be 4,355 (or whatever).

Give the applicant an opportunity to practice several minutes on the typewriter to be used for the test. The test copy for the applicant should not show the line stroke totals. They should appear only on the master copy which is used for scoring. A speed test usually is ten minutes long. Give the starting and finishing signals.

To grade the test follow these five steps:

(1) Jot down the total strokes typed.

(2) Divide the total strokes by five (average number of strokes per word) to get the gross number of words typed.

(3) Divide the gross number by ten (ten-minute test) to get the gross number of words per minute.

(4) Count the errors. Proofread the test copy carefully, placing a circle around every misspelled word, omitted punctuation, omitted word, strikeover, and so forth. Count the circles for the total errors.

(5) Subtract the total number of errors from the gross number of words per minute in (3) above to get the net number of words per minute.

Suppose an applicant typed 2,980 strokes in ten minutes with five errors. The computation, according to the five steps above, would be as follows:

(1) 2,980 strokes

(2) 596 gross number of words typed in ten minutes (2,980 divided by 5)

(3) 59.6 or 60 gross number of words per minute (596 divided by 10)

(4) 5 errors

(5) 55 net number of words per minute (60 minus 5)

A typing score of 40–50 words per minute is fair; 50–60 is good; above 60 is above average. Give the applicant another test if he thinks he can improve his score.

To give a shorthand test, dictate to the applicant two or more

100–150 word letters prepared for this purpose. The letters should compare with the kind normally dictated. The supervisor may need to practice his dictation speed to make it between 80–100 words per minute. He might time himself on the following 100-word letter. (Include inside address).

Dr. Harold Jones
Denomination College
College Town, USA

DEAR DR. JONES:

I accept your kind invitation to speak to the students and faculty on October 6 on the occasion of the college's twentieth anniversary.

Thank you for sending along a copy of the latest yearbook. I reviewed it with a great deal of interest, especially since three of our own young people are students at Denomination College.

Your willingness to meet me at the airport is certainly appreciated. However, Mrs. Gregory and I plan to make the trip by car.

I'm looking forward to this assignment. Thanks for asking me.

Sincerely,

Observe the applicant's shorthand speed and general ability. Assign a typewriter and request a transcription of notes. Record elapsed time for the transcription. Divide the total number of minutes into the total number of words dictated to get an average words-per-minute score. A score of 15–25 words-per-minute is average.

Observe also the finished product—the typed letters. Are they framed well on the page? Is the left margin even? Is the right margin fairly even? Are there strikeovers or messy erasures? Would one be willing to sign his name to these letters for mailing?

Give the applicant an opportunity to try again if the first transcription test is not acceptable. A strange environment often keeps a person from performing at his best.

One may wish to assign the giving and scoring of typing tests to a secretary in the office. Perhaps the dictator should give the shorthand test.

Select the Qualified Applicant

To evaluate the qualifications of people is a fine art and requires a high order of judgment. In some instances it is clear, after interviewing two or three applicants, which person is most acceptable. In other instances, when applicants have similar qualifications, the decision is more difficult to make. The interviewer may base his decision on positive reactions resulting from the overall screening process.

He may ask himself questions such as: Who is best qualified skillwise? Who would fit in best with the other office workers? Who seems to be most alert? Who has the best ability to express himself? Who seems most self-confident? Who seems to have the best health?

A good supervisor makes every effort to eliminate personal prejudice from his employment decisions. A few of the common prejudices are color of hair, posture, eyes close together, protruding chin, large ears, the way the hair is cut or groomed.

Prejudice usually creeps into one's personality makeup so gradually he is suprised to learn of its presence. A person should study his areas of prejudice. They may be a hindrance to the intelligent selection of people for jobs in the church.

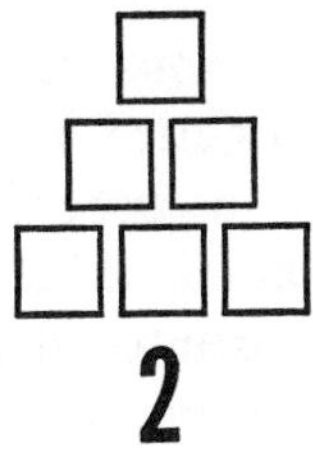

2

Helping the New Staff Member Get a Good Start

Most people have either pleasant or unpleasant memories of their first day on a job. If one had an unpleasant experience, chances are he would feel, upon reflection, that his frustrations could easily have been avoided if better induction planning had been done by the supervisor.

For example, when one minister of education was asked to relate his first day's experience, he said:

"The pastor was out of the city in a revival meeting. I didn't know my way around and was not even sure of the location of my office. Much of that first day I spent walking through the church facilities. I introduced myself to the janitors, the maid, and met the workers in the church offices. But I wasn't sure which persons, if any, I would supervise. Of course when the pastor returned, he showed me around and answered my questions. Since then he has given me excellent counsel, help, and support. But I'll never forget the frustrations I felt that first day."

Another staff worker had a different reaction: "I recall the first day as a very pleasant experience. The pastor took time to give me a personally conducted tour of the church buildings and grounds as well as of the church's mission. He introduced me to all the workers, then showed me my office which was clean and ready to move into. After lunch together we spent two hours in the pastor's office. He showed me the church staff organization chart, reviewed my job, and explained my supervisory responsibilities. I felt that I got off to a good start."

Although a supervisor on a church staff remembers how important induction days were to him, he sometimes forgets or overlooks their importance to subsequent new workers whom he is to supervise.

When a newly employed person arrives for work on the first day, he should be treated courteously and be made to feel at ease. He wants to be welcomed to a job—not thrown into it. A new worker usually comes to the job with keen anticipation—a desire to give his best. The supervisor's role is to stimulate, not to deflate.

When asked to recall their first day at work, several office workers made these comments:

"My first day was pleasant. The supervisor introduced me to all the workers and arranged for one of the girls to go on break and to lunch with me. He showed me my work place and got me started."

"The supervisor showed me my desk and then excused himself for a conference. I sat there like a log for three hours with nothing to do. I tried to look busy. I finally got a *Young People's Quarterly* and started typing one of the lessons. Was I ever frustrated!"

"From the very first day my supervisor has never called me by my right name."

"On the first day he led me to believe I would get a salary increase in six months. I finally got one after fourteen months."

"I was made to feel wanted and needed. The supervisor talked to me as if he had all day, and I know he had loads of work to do. He was friendly, helpful, and interested in my making good on the job."

A good program of employee induction—helping the new worker get a good start—should provide a thorough introduction to the overall work of the church so that he may understand the framework in which he operates. Whether for new professional, clerical, or janitorial paid staff members, the induction program should include:

- A tour of the church's facilities
- An introduction to all staff workers
- An explanation of employee benefits
- Complete information of the church's personnel policies, procedures, salary program, pay dates, work hours, and so forth
- A review and explanation of job duties
- Information as to how the paid staff is organized to carry out the church's functions
- A brief review of the church's history

The supervisor who plans well for the arrival of a new worker arranges his own work schedule to allow ample time for unhurried and uninterrupted talks.

The supervisor who says "I don't have that much time to give to a new worker" should reflect further upon his responsibility as a supervisor. He is the logical person to induct new employees. Other people may come into the picture incidentally, but he is mainly responsible for getting the new worker started right. If inducted by a peer, the new worker may think that he is not very important or that the job is not too important. He may even question who his supervisor is.

The question, Who is my supervisor? may be the beginning of a future problem. When the new worker needs help on the job, he may go to the person who inducted him rather than to his supervisor. He is still trying to understand the induction actions of the supervisor who said "I don't want to be bothered." It may take several months for the supervisor to break down some of the feeling barriers he built during an ill-planned induction.

A day or so before the new employee reports for work be sure that his office and desk are clean. The desk should be stocked with an assortment of supplies neatly arranged. A new worker should not be expected to clean the desk or work space of a former employee.

The overall conservation of time, effort, and cost, through a program of planned induction and training of new employees, makes supervision a challenge indeed.

An induction program usually covers two or three weeks. Below is a suggested schedule. Some of the suggestions may not be pertinent to all concerned, but they may help to develop individual plans—one for the professional members and one for the office and manual paid staff workers.

First Day

- Be in the office when the new worker arrives.
- Greet him cordially and make him feel welcome.
- Assist him to complete forms required to place him on the payroll—such as income tax, insurance, hospitalization, pension, and so forth.
- Explain the salary program and pay dates.
- Introduce him to all staff members.
- Take him on a tour of the church's facilities; show him where to park his car.
- Show him his office or work place and where to hang his hat and coat.
- Explain the day's work schedule including rest breaks, lunch hour, and so forth.
- Review his duties and give him a copy of his job description.
- Show him the organization chart of the paid staff and how his job is related to the total staff work. Give him a copy.
- Get him started on his job; show how it should be done and tell him why. Give him an opportunity to ask questions.
- Follow up with him later in the day.

Second Day

- Give him an opportunity to ask questions about the previous day's activities.
- Review the employee benefit program. This might include benefits such as vacation, holidays, pension, hospitalization, in-

surance, revival meetings, attendance at state and convention-wide meetings, housing allowance, car expense.

- Explain the church's personnel policies and procedures.

End of the First Week

- Give him an opportunity to ask for further information or clarification of his duties.
- Explain how the church is organized to perform its work. Include church committees as well as the educational organizations.
- Review briefly the church's history.
- Check employee's work. Commend and instruct as appropriate.

First Paycheck

- Hand him his first paycheck; explain the deductions.
- Discuss his work progress. Ask how he thinks he is getting along. Answer his questions. Give constructive help.
- Give him a chance to share his ideas about how certain tasks may be done. Some of the best ideas for work and facility improvements come from new workers.

After the first paycheck, then what? Is the new employee now on his own? What other responsibilities, if any, does the supervisor have to the new worker?

On the Job Training

Actually, a supervisor's job to train others is never finished. The first six months for a new employee are most important. He learns many things. He develops good or bad work habits. A good supervisor is always close by to encourage, commend, counsel, and instruct. His role is to help people develop their potential.

As the weeks and months pass, the supervisor should continue to observe the work of all those for whom he is responsible and to take whatever remedial action is necessary. The supervisor should:

- Observe such things as repeated tardiness, frequent absence, failure to adhere to rest period and lunch hour schedules. Infractions are usually indicators of job disinterest, personal or home problems.
- Check quality as well as quantity of work performed.
- Check work habits.
- Discuss work problems at the time they occur.
- Encourage improvement.
- Make every effort to be available when the worker desires council.

Good supervisors know that a plan for induction, training, and follow-through drastically reduces the time needed by new employees to become skilful and productive. A good induction program has other benefits:

- Reduces turnover; new employees do not get discouraged and quit.
- Develops in the workers a sense of pride to be associated with the church.
- Gives workers a feeling of confidence.
- Develops morale.
- Provides status and recognition.
- Builds teamwork.

However, now and then a person on the staff develops a poor attitude, is uncooperative and difficult to work with, and turns out shoddy work.

A good case for dismissal? Before a conclusion is reached, a person should review his role of supervisor.

He is responsible for the performance of his workers, for helping them to attain their highest possible potential. Along with this responsibility goes commensurate authority to properly and reasonably direct and stimulate the workers to perform their jobs as efficiently as possible.

Workers who are allowed to fail in their tasks can never be used by the supervisor as an alibi. The responsibility for getting the job done rests more on him than on the worker.

When lack of interest, unrest, poor performance, tardiness,

absenteeism, or other faults are evident, the supervisor must take immediate action to correct these failings or take alternate steps to dismiss the worker.

For example, assume a dismissal situation. Over a period of months each instance of job failure had been discussed with the worker. Further, the supervisor communicated unmistakably that he expected immediate improvement. Assume, also, that the worker did understand that his work performance was not satisfactory. Based upon these assumptions, termination may be the best solution.

However, some situations not involving work fault may require immediate dismissal. Such offenses include theft, dishonesty, and falsification of records.

Suggested steps leading to termination are as follows:

- Discuss the matter thoroughly with the pastor. Go over the file of recorded work faults and related conferences. The file should include incidents, violations, remedial conferences held, and dates. The pastor and supervisor may wish to discuss the matter with the personnel committee. Such a conference is recommended.
- Set the date for dismissal. Invite the chairman or a member of the personnel committee to the meeting. Do not notify the worker in advance of the date. He may become a greater problem by trying to secure the sympathy of other workers and of some church members.
- Arrange to have the worker's check ready on the date set for dismissal. Additional pay—two weeks or more—is usually included in the final paycheck.
- Late in the afternoon on the date of dismissal the supervisor should call the worker into his office. He is responsible for telling the worker of the decision. In most cases, after proper remedial action has been taken throughout the work history of the employee, he is not too surprised when told of his dismissal. The worker receives the check. He is terminated at once.
- Explaining the dismissal action to the other workers the following day may or may not be necessary. They usually know

the reason, and any additional reference to it may make them think, "Maybe I'm next."

Some Termination "Do's and "Don't's"

Do invite the chairman or a member of the personnel committee to be present.

Do state clearly and briefly the purpose of the meeting.

Do review briefly the history of the employee's work habits leading to dismissal.

Do remain firm in your decision, even though he pleads for another chance—assuming he has had previous opportunities.

Do be calm and maintain your poise.

Do try to keep the goodwill of the employee.

Do explain the additional severance pay, if any.

Do be extremely careful what you say if the reason for dismissal is based on moral behavior.

Do give the employee an opportunity to talk.

Don't get into an argument.

Don't permit him to bring into the conversation names of other staff workers.

Don't "talk down" to the person.

Don't extend the meeting any longer than necessary.

Dismissing a worker is an unpleasant task. There are times however, when the church, through its staff, must take this final action.

Dismissal may be the most helpful thing the church can do for the individual. Usually, when a worker fails, the church also has failed to some degree. So, whenever possible, try to change a poor worker into a good worker. This is one reward of good supervision.

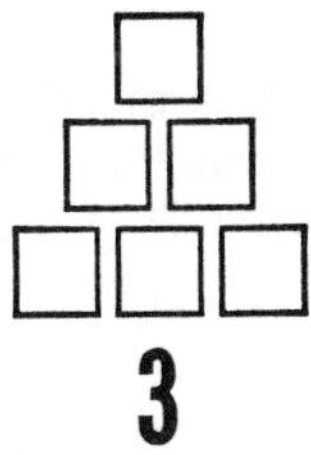

3

Organizing to Get the Job Done

No staff member works in isolation. The entire staff is mutually dependant in achieving both group and individual work goals.

However, some church staff workers seem to prefer a sort of isolationism. They plan and promote their own work separately from church goals. Their attitude appears to be one of "you take care of your work and I'll take care of mine." They never quite understand how their work is related to the total group effort. They come and go as they please. No one knows where they are. They usually want to be excused from staff meetings. Resulting schedule and work conflicts are a common occurrence.

The "lone wolf" attitude is sometimes prompted and encouraged by being in an isolated or separated office.

Sometimes, a particular professional employee on the church staff is highly skilled in his work and is allowed to be a team misfit for the sake of his skill. As problems arise, staff workers are asked to indulge the strange actions and idiocyncracies of the team's recalcitrant member. What a price for the other staff members to pay! In time, if the situation remains unchanged, group harmony and unity disintegrate.

The concept of a group working together to accomplish its

goals requires teamwork—everyday teamwork from every staff member.

For example, one worker may be assigned the task of gathering, editing, and typing materials for the weekly bulletin. Usually, these materials do not magically appear on the worker's desk at precisely the same predetermined time each week. The weekly ritual involves reminding staff workers of copy due, or working with them to clarify, expand, or cut copy. In some churches a second person may be responsible to type copy after it has been gathered and edited. Still another person may be assigned to operate the addressing machine, stuff and mail the printed or duplicated bulletins. Failure of one person to meet established deadlines at any point in the process impairs efficiency and, if allowed to continue, reduces group morale. Conversely, if every step in gathering, editing, typing, and mailing the weekly bulletin moves according to schedule, the team feels that "we are organized" in the total effort.

What Is Organization?

An organization is formed whenever two or more people come together to achieve common goals.

The pastor and one paid worker—regular or regular-part-time—form an organization. Both are involved in it. The situation is similar to that of the farmer who, when his city cousin asked what time he went to work said "Go to work? Man, I wake up in the middle of it!"

Some staff members never quite get into the "middle of it." Their noticeable unconcern and shoddy work habits indicate a periphery interest at best. A person's name on a roster identifies him as a worker on the team but not necessarily as a team worker.

A church staff may comprise two, five, ten, twenty, or more workers. The larger the staff the more a good organization becomes an absolute necessity in order to get the job done.

What is an organization like? The three blind men expressed three different concepts in describing an elephant. Their answers were based upon the encounter they had with it. A staff supervisor's concept of an organization depends upon his encounter with it.

One might say, "It's like a heavy weight or burden." This description represents the viewpoint of the supervisor who does not know how to delegate the many details of his work. He does not use available human resources. For him an organization is a heavy burden.

Another staff supervisor describes his encounter, "An organization is like a cloud that comes and goes." To him an organization is an elusive thing, here today, gone tomorrow. He may ask: Where is that committee that was organized six months ago? When was our purchasing procedure changed? What happened to that special project that was set up three months ago?

Yet another supervisor might say, "An organization is like an empty house." From his viewpoint and experience an organization exists as a framework loosely put together, the foundation and supports not being too important. To him the significant thing is to get something started—anything. Consequently, some projects flourish for a while and then die, leaving nothing behind but emptiness.

A good organization is not represented by any of these viewpoints. Nor is it an object one can see. One characteristic of a good organization is that it operates so smoothly and efficiently that the staff members are scarcely aware of its existence.

An organization evolves when goals are determined and functions defined. Organization involves grouping related activities and setting up lines of authority.

The purpose of organization is to bring order, system, and arrangement of functions into being. It serves to bind people together as they move in the same direction to achieve common goals.

However, organization for the sake of organization does not necessarily guarantee good performance. Peter F. Drucker states: "Good organization by itself does not produce good performance. . . . But poor organization makes good performance impossible." If the church staff is to match good performance with good organization, cooperation and teamwork are required of every worker. Good performance requires living together with mutual respect shown for one another's personality and ability. A church staff is a social phenomonon.

The Advantages of Good Organization

Good staff organization helps a church to:

- Accomplish program goals
- Define, group, and assign activities and duties related to goals to the workers so they can perform their jobs effectively
- Develop lay leadership
- Offer greater opportunities for the spiritual development of the members
- Achieve unity of purpose and teamwork action

A church staff may be well organized and yet not function properly. The crucial factor is the quality of the supervision. A poor organization with poor supervision is intolerable. A good organization with poor supervision is little better. A good organization with good supervision usually gets the job done. Interestingly enough, a good supervisor working in a poor organizational structure may yet get acceptable performance and production mainly because of his leadership skills. In time if nothing is done to improve the overall church staff organization, the good supervisor tends to optimize production in his own area by reviewing and rewriting job descriptions and work procedures, or by rearranging facilities to accommodate better work flow. How much better it is for the personnel committee and the pastor to initiate the reorganization project to the end that the entire staff benefits.

Reorganizing the Church Staff

In an established church it is not necessary to set up a *new* staff organization. An organization already exists. The church's interest is mainly one of staff reorganization.

At least three restraining influences must be dealt with in reorganizing a church staff:

• The first exists because of the personalities and characteristics of the workers presently on the staff. Through the years one or more positions may have had tasks added from time to time, and the workers now claim "squatter's rights." This attitude often precludes a worker's full cooperation in a restudy and redistribution of work assignments. Also some workers from the very beginning of their tenure develop a strange work philosophy—their job belongs to them, not to the church. Or, perhaps, a marginal worker was employed years ago as a stenographer when job skills were not considered too important. In the beginning her work may have been acceptable. But with an increased staff and greater demands for output, her lack of skill is now a liability. Consequently, if those in charge of the reorganization study wish to retain her because of tenure of service or some other reason, they must decide either to live with her inefficiency as a steno, or to reassign her to a staff job she can perform.

• The second restraining influence exists because casual work habits have been developed by employees over a period of time. Work production has gradually deteriorated to a "low gear" operation. The workers are accustomed to certain work habits and do not want to be disturbed. These are the workers who, when a work crisis occurs, usually cry for extra help instead of moving into a "pulling gear." Even new workers, who at first were enthusiastic and anxious to produce at their maximum, finally succumb to the "low gear" routine.

Generally, the cause of an easy going work force is ineffective supervision. Some supervisors are completely oblivious to the problem. They think they are running a "taut ship." Their only standard for comparison is their own work habits.

The church sometimes causes the problem by employing a full-time person for only half-time work to assist a professional worker. The half-time worker has ample time to socialize, to take extended rest breaks and lunch hours. This situation ultimately affects the work habits and attitudes of others on the staff.

• The third restriction is economic. The reorganization study may reveal the necessity for adding one or more staff workers, or the need to upgrade the church's salary program. The question is: Can the church afford the possible salary increase cost? Some churches discover that, even though nominal salary increases have been given year after year, they still have not been sufficient to keep up with rising salaries in the community. This revelation usually comes as a shock.

Conversely, what effect will a restudy and reassignment of job duties have on salary rates in job descriptions? A reorganization study may result in lowering the salary rates in some job descriptions and raising them in others. What effect will such a restudy have on the workers? Where economic matters are involved, employees may prefer to keep their present job status rather than to risk the unknown, unless they are assured that there will be no salary reduction even though some jobs may be downgraded.

Steps in the Reorganization Process

The purpose of a paid staff is to serve in a supporting role as the church strives to attain its goals. The staff members perform those supportive duties to maintain ongoing church activities and programs. Some church programs and activities would bog down if it were not for the clerical detail performed behind the scenes. Clean facilities not only add greatly to the comfort of church members but also help provide a setting conducive to worship. The following steps are suggested as a guide in a restudy of staff organization:

- Identify the staff's functions. Group the work under several headings such as preaching and pastoral ministry, education and music ministry, office-clerical, and facility maintenance.
- Divide the total work load of each function into manageable parts. In the office-clerical function, for example, write down every task which must be performed to support the church's goals. The list may number fifty items or more. Do not include tasks that church members can and should perform. See Exhibit VI for a partial listing.
- Group related activities. In a smaller church the wise and economical course may be to combine two or more areas of work

in one job description until such time as church growth requires another worker. See chapter 4 for suggestions in writing job descriptions.

• Assign responsibility. One of the most important steps in implementing good organization is to communicate job assignments and responsibility clearly and accurately. Communication is the perennial task of the staff supervisor. His ability to gain worker acceptance is a determining factor in the success of a reorganization undertaking. Mutual respect and confidence must prevail. Usually, the worker is willing to cooperate when he understands that the purpose of good organization is to help him perform his job more efficiently.

• Avoid overlapping responsibility. Do the job description statements clearly differentiate one job from another? Or will the employees wonder at times who is to do what and when? Each job must be clearly defined.

In one church, the task "operate the duplicating machine" was included as a regular duty on five different job descriptions. The church, in its effort to gain flexibility, created confusion instead. Not only was the duplicating machine frequently out of order and supplies out of stock, but the duplicating room usually looked as if a tornado had passed through.

In another church, the minister of education and the pastor both agreed verbally to make hospital calls. However, they had to hold frequent meetings to determine who was going to visit whom and when.

In still another church an out-of-city guest, who saw several clerical workers in one office area, asked the supervisor what their different jobs were. The supervisor replied, "Well, we all do everything that comes up. We are a great team. Right, girls?" The weak smiles and harried looks on the workers' faces resembled people looking forward to their exit from a stuck elevator.

• Identify levels of supervision. In a smaller church the pastor may be the only supervisor of all the paid workers. As the church staff grows in number and reorganization is studied and implemented, the pastor should share the supervisory responsibilities with one or more professional workers. This is known as delegation. It is sharing authority. By so doing, the pastor activates the organization structure that he and the personnel committee planned.

A pastor may insist on supervising directly every new worker who joins the staff. In time he will find that he not only does not have enough hours in the day to perform his own work, but that he is creating more work and personnel problems for himself and the other staff members. The best solution is for the pastor to set up levels of supervision by grouping related job descriptions. For example, the clerical workers whose jobs are related to record, stenographic, and finance duties (and sometimes the maintenance workers) may be assigned to the minister of education or to the church business administrator. The paid education age-group workers, such as children, youth, and adult directors, should be assigned to the minister of education; the organist to the minister of music. See Exhibit V for sample organization charts. Every church is a different situation and must vary its supervisory assignments accordingly.

The important point is that every worker on the staff should report to one supervisor only. Nothing is more frustrating to a worker than not knowing who his supervisor is, unless it is to feel that he has too many of them.

Try this experiment: If as many as ten people are on the staff, ask each one to write the name of his supervisor. The results may cause chagrin. Some may write the name of the chairman of the personnel committee, or the "church"; others the pastor's name (he may or may not be); still others may name two people, including, perhaps, the name of another clerical worker. When incorrect answers are given, it becomes evident that communication efforts have been about as effective as the sign "wet paint."

Each worker must know who his supervisor is, and he must know that the worker knows. This is a cardinal rule underlying an effective organizational structure.

• **Maintain a reasonable span of control.** Span of control

EXHIBIT V

CHURCH STAFF ORGANIZATION CHARTS (Samples)

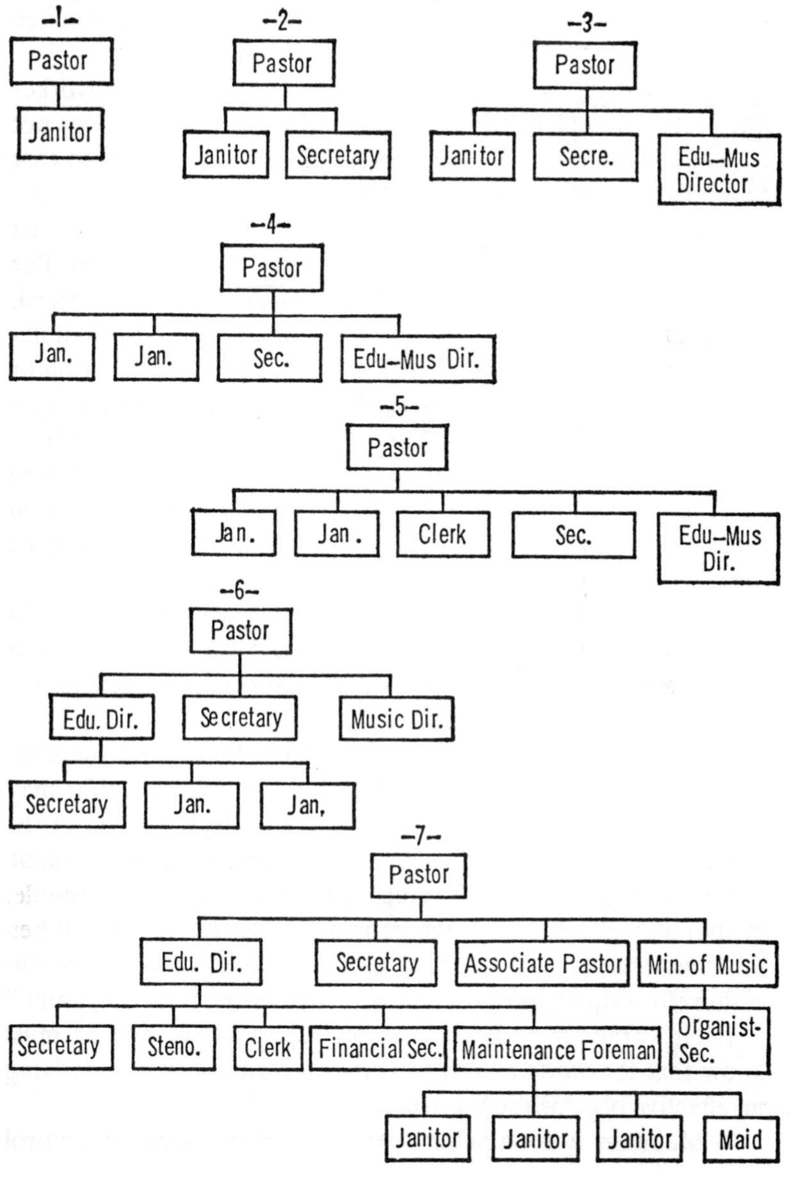

PAST

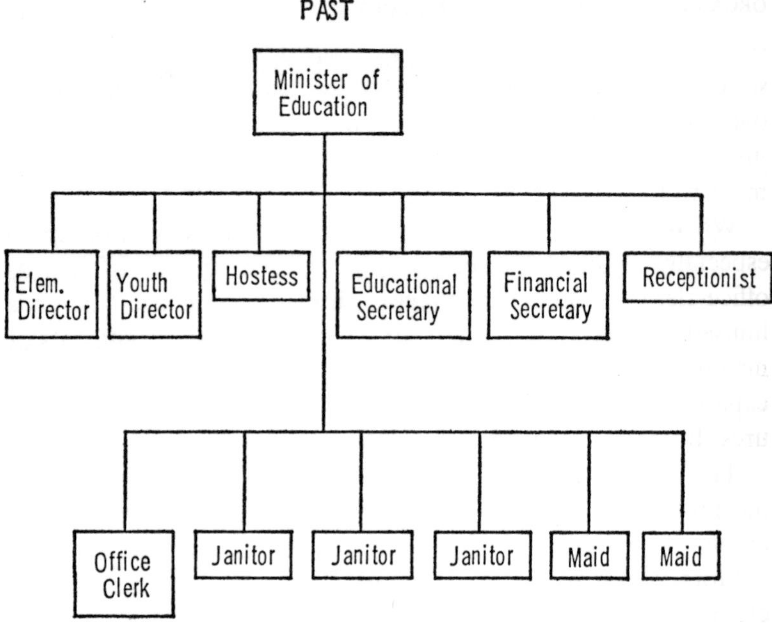

REVISED

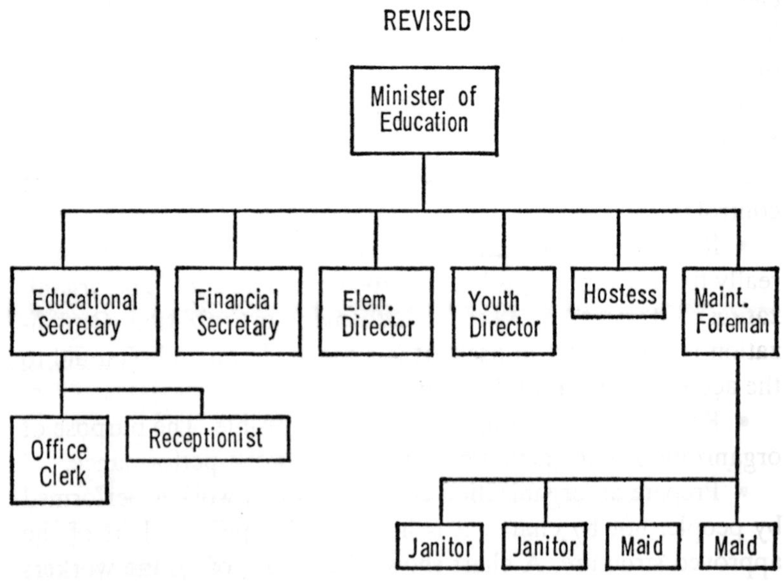

refers to the number of people supervised by any one person. To set up supervision lines too thin—one over one over one (pastor over one professional worker over one clerical worker)—may be just as undesirable as for the pastor to supervise directly all ten or more workers on a church staff.

When a person supervises more than ten or twelve workers—especially if they represent several different functions such as office-clerical, maintenance, age-group workers, music—he finds himself with no time to perform the professional assignments of his own job. He is spread too thin. As a result, some extremely capable and qualified staff supervisors have been dubbed failures. Instead, they were victims of poor organizational structure.

The solution to an extremely wide span of control is to explore the possibility of creating another level of supervision. For example, the minister of education who directs the work of three janitors, two maids, and one church hostess in addition to four clerical and two age-group workers may decide, after study, that the best approach is to create two new jobs: a maintenance foreman over the janitors and maids, and a secretary over the clerical workers. The new jobs might be filled by present workers if they are qualified, thus eliminating the need for an expansion of personnel.

The past and revised organization charts might appear as shown on page 40.

An organization chart shows levels of supervision and span of control of each.

• Keep the organization flexible. An organization is never really fixed. Rather, it is both a process and a result. The organization chart is a "still shot" of a changing organization. Organization is not an end in itself. It is a means to an end—an aid to the accomplishment of the church's goals.

• Keep the organization as simple as possible. The purpose of organization is to facilitate, not hamper work performance.

• Prepare an organization chart. Although work is performed by people, not by charts, it is helpful to prepare a chart of the approved structure. A chart shows the names of all the workers

—regular and regular part-time—and their job titles, the names of the supervisors and the workers who report to them, those who are on the same peer levels, and work relationships. Date the chart and give each worker a copy. Explain its purpose and use.

Responsibility of Reorganizing a Church Staff

The pastor and the personnel committee work together on this project. The process of reorganization requires an objective attitude. Best results are not attained if one or more committee members allow personal feelings, bias, or prejudice to color decisions and actions.

The workers should be informed of the project. A good time to do this is when they are asked to cooperate in filling in their own job questionnaire forms. Experience shows that when workers are involved in the process and have contributed to it, they will strive to make the implementation of the reorganization successful.

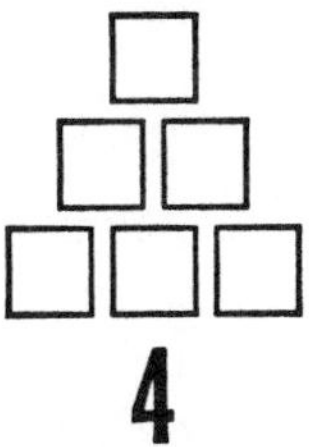

4

Assigning Tasks to Workers

Every church has job descriptions of a sort. They may be written, or they may exist only in someone's mind. When unwritten, a staff member may not be sure of his exact responsibilities. New assignments added from time to time may have expanded his job during the years. A real problem occurs when such a worker terminates. Written job descriptions identify responsibility.

Regardless of size, every church has many and varied tasks that must be performed regularly or periodically. In a smaller church, the pastor may do all the clerical work that is required. Sometimes church members voluntarily perform services such as janitorial work, maintenance of the church membership roll, and office work. In a larger church several paid staff workers perform varied tasks. They answer the telephone, take and transcribe dictation, operate the duplicating machine, type educational records, keep financial records, file correspondence, clean the buildings—to name only a few of the tasks. See Exhibit VI for a more complete list of tasks.

The term "job description" refers to an organized summary of the duties and responsibilities involved in a position such as pastor, minister of education, minister of music, business admin-

Exhibit VI
A List of Some *of the Tasks Performed in a Church*

1. Maintain up-to-date mailing lists
2. Take and transcribe dictation
3. Operate addressograph
4. Operate duplicating machine
5. Cut stencils
6. Type form letters
7. Type organizational record cards
8. Maintain an orderly stock and duplicating room
9. Stuff and seal envelopes
10. Answer the telephone
11. Make telephone calls to choir officers, committee members, and various other people as assigned
12. Maintain petty cash fund
13. Requisition and maintain office supplies
14. Check organization attendance records
15. Edit copy for church bulletin
16. Compile monthly organizational records
17. Figure time cards
18. Order supplies
19. Order literature each quarter
20. Book and clear meetings on date book
21. Assist in preparing education budget
22. File general correspondence
23. Maintain file of special promotional programs
24. Enlist teachers for study course
25. Enlist education workers
26. Maintain visitation file
27. Maintain roll of church members
28. Act as office receptionist
29. Play organ for all church services
30. Maintain music files
31. Plan meals, purchase food, and supervise meal preparation and service.
32. Plan for and promote organizational growth and efficiency
33. Organize and promote a churchwide visitation program
34. Direct the various choirs and lead congregational singing
35. Supervise the work of others
36. Plan recreational activities
37. Train pianists and choristers

38. Execute church-approved personnel policies
39. Count offering, make deposits
40. Post distribution of budget receipts
41. Compile and type monthly financial reports
42. Post tithes and offerings to individual member accounts
43. Mail individual tithe and offering reports to members
44. Compose and type routine letters
45. Type sermons
46. Make travel reservations
47. Perform general office work
48. Review, open, digest, and distribute mail
49. Sweep, mop, buff, clean, and wax floors
50. Operate heating and cooling equipment

istrator, maintenance supervisor, organist, stenographer, secretary, financial secretary, janitor, maid, and hostess.

Usually, two different forms are used in securing information and writing job descriptions. They are (1) the job questionnaire form and (2) the job description form. See Exhibits VII and VIII for suggested forms.

The purpose of job descriptions is to give an overall concept of the tasks performed in each position and to show how each differs from the others. Job descriptions make it possible to present a great deal of organized, pertinent information about each position quickly and concisely. See pages 59–75 for a more detailed discussion of the purposes and values of job descriptions.

Preparing to Write Job Descriptions

The following steps are suggested:

• Decide to do it. The pastor and the personnel committee should give leadership to the project. Usually, a subcommittee, composed of one or more members of the personnel committee and one or two members of the church staff, is desirable. The pastor should serve on the committee. His leadership will help to assure its acceptance by the other staff members and will give successful implementation to the project.

• Agree on the work scope of the job description committee.

EXHIBIT VII

POSITION QUESTIONNAIRE FORM

________________________________ Church

Present Job Title ______________________ Date ______________

Name of Supervisor ______________________ Prepared by __________

1. PRINCIPAL FUNCTION:

2. REGULAR DUTIES: (List the major duties that your job normally requires you to perform)

3. OTHER DUTIES: (List the duties you perform that are not on a regular basis)

(Please complete reverse side)

EXHIBIT VII

POSITION QUESTIONNAIRE FORM

(page 2)

The following questions are intended to clarify the special skills, knowledge, and experience required to fulfil the normal requirements of the job.

4. WHAT KIND OF OFFICE EQUIPMENT DO YOU USE?

(Machine or Equipment) (Used occasionally, frequently, continuously)

5. WHAT SKILLS DOES THIS JOB REQUIRE? (Such as typing, shorthand, proofreading, filing, etc.)

6. DOES THIS JOB REQUIRE

(1) assigning routine work to others?____________________
(2) or, giving direct supervision to others?____________________
List names of those directly supervised, if any____________________

____

7. WHAT DECISIONS DO YOU NORMALLY MAKE IN THIS POSITION WITHOUT GETTING APPROVAL?

(Nature of the Decision) (Frequency of Occurrence)

8. WHAT CONTACTS DO YOU MAKE WITH PEOPLE OUTSIDE THE CHURCH?

(Printers, vendors, etc.)

9. ADDITIONAL COMMENTS (Which will help to describe your job completely)

10. PLEASE WRITE WHAT YOU CONSIDER IS THE MAIN PURPOSE OF YOUR JOB

EXHIBIT VIII

POSITION DESCRIPTION FORM

______________________________________Church

Job Title______________________________________Date_______________

1. PRINCIPAL FUNCTION:

2. REGULAR DUTIES:

3. OTHER DUTIES:

4. REQUIRED JOB QUALIFICATIONS:

Education
Experience
Skills

This is outlined by the full personnel committee. In brief, the subcommittee addresses itself to these tasks: (1) determine the method of securing job information from the workers; (2) design the job questionnaire and job description forms; (3) analyze the completed questionnaires for clarity, completeness, and correctness; (4) write the job descriptions; and (5) assist in implementing the project.

• Prepare the questionnaire and job description forms. Keep them simple. Workers usually lose some of their interest when they have more than two pages of questions to answer.

• Conduct conferences with the staff members. The pastor should preside and explain the purpose of the project. In a large church, it may be desirable to have two or three separate meetings, one for professional staff members, such as minister of education, minister of music, director of youth work, one for the clerical workers, and another for the maintenance workers. The purpose of divided meetings is to give the workers more freedom to ask questions concerning details of the project.

Distribute copies of the job questionnaire to the workers during the conference. Show how the information requested on the questionnaire is necessary in order to write the final job description. Read aloud each statement on the questionnaire. Give opportunity for questions. Explain the method to be used in securing questionnaire information. See (a) and (b) below.

Getting Job Description Facts

The purpose of the job questionnaire is to get specific facts from each person about his job—what he does and what skills are involved.

These specific facts are secured by one of two methods: (a) requesting each individual to fill in a job questionnaire; or, (b) interviewing the workers individually to get job information.

The first method (a) usually requires less time for the completion of all the questionnaires. When using this method, request each worker to list first the duty which he considers to be most frequently performed, then list the remaining duties in descending order of frequency. Give the workers at least a week to complete their job questionnaires.

The second method (b) requires one or more personal interviews with each worker included in the job description survey. The worker's supervisor or a member of the personnel committee may conduct the interview. The interviewer asks the questions listed on the questionnaire, then writes in the worker's answers. The worker's responses may elicit from the interviewer other related and pertinent questions, not on the questionnaire but helpful in grasping the full content and scope of the job. List only the skills that the job requires, such as typing, shorthand, filing. Do not list a skill that a worker may possess but which is not required to perform the job.

Either method of securing job information, (a) or (b), is acceptable. However, method (a) has some distinct advantages: the worker by filling in his own form at a time most convenient to him, does not feel pushed or hurried; there is less chance of omitting important tasks when an employee has opportunity to mull over his work assignments.

The person conducting the interview should be careful not to question the worker's statements of job duties. The purpose of preparing a job questionnaire is to report as accurately as possible each job as it presently exists. Analyzing the questionnaries and comparing duties with other jobs will come later.

One word of caution may be appropriate. Occasionally, a worker may make his job appear more important than it really is. The converse may be true also. Every job on the staff is important and needed; the church would not needlessly spend money for salary and employee benefits. Those who analyze the completed questionnaires must weigh each job statement carefully and in context with the statements on all other related jobs.

Sometimes, regardless of the method used in securing job information, the worker is not always certain as to the amount of time normally spent on each task. In such instances another helpful tool, "Job Time Analysis Chart," may be effectively used. See Exhibit IX for a suggested "Job Time Analysis" form.

EXHIBIT IX

Job Time Analysis Chart

Name ______________________________ Date ____________

____

Time	Duties Performed
8:00 - 8:15	
8:15 - 8:30	
8:30 - 8:45	
8:45 - 9:00	
9:00 - 9:15	
9:15 - 9:30	
9:30 - 9:45	
9:45 -10:00	
10:00 -10:15	
10:15 -10:30	
10:30 -10:45	
10:45 -11:00	
11:00 -11:15	
11:15 -11:30	
11:30 -11:45	
4:00 - 4:15	
4:15 - 4:30	

To use this chart, ask each worker to keep an accurate time record of the different duties performed each day for at least two weeks. Provide a space on the time chart by each fifteen-minute time interval to write in the task or tasks performed.

After two weeks of maintaining the time chart, request each worker to prepare a summary of the total time spent on the various duties and list them according to time totals. Then figure the percentage of each task's time against the total time for all tasks. The results of a two-week job time analysis (80 hours) by an office worker may resemble the following summary:

Duty	*Time*	*Percent*
1. Process educational records	20 hours, 10 minutes	25.53
2. Answer the telephone	15 hours, 15 minutes	19.30
3. Take and transcribe dictation	8 hours, 30 minutes	10.76
4. Type copy for duplication	6 hours, 15 minutes	7.91
5. Stuff bulletins for mailing	6 hours	7.59
6. Stamping mail	3 hours, 10 minutes	4.01
7. Receive visitors and members	2 hours, 45 minutes	3.48
8. Rest periods	2 hours, 30 minutes	3.16
9. Type church bulletin copy	2 hours, 10 minutes	2.74
10. Receive and distribute mail	2 hours	2.53
11. Address envelopes	2 hours	2.53
12. Call members for committee meetings	1 hour, 50 minutes	2.32
13. Filing	1 hour, 40 minutes	2.11
14. Look for the janitor	1 hour, 35 minutes	2.00
15. Operate duplicating machine	1 hour	1.27
16. Type form letters to new church members	45 minutes	.95
17. Rearrange stock and supplies in duplicating room	35 minutes	.73
18. Look for lost articles for members who call in	25 minutes	.54
19. Missed bus; late for work	25 minutes	.54

Although the faithful maintenance of a job time analysis study may seem tedious, the results make such an effort worthwhile. The chart is helpful to the worker. Guesswork about duties performed is largely eliminated, especially as it pertains to time spent on each of the various duties. For example, it is quite possible for a worker who dislikes to answer the telephone to feel that a large portion of time is spent in this activity. The time chart may show that the telephone is answered only six or eight times a day.

Supported with facts, the worker now is better able to complete the job questionnaire accurately. Also, the recorded day-to-day activities of the several workers may reveal to the personnel committee job inequities, unnecessary work duplication, lost work time, or a need to reassign some of the duties to other persons.

For best results, plan the job time analysis during a normal period of operation.

Review with the individual the completed information on the job questionnaire. This is important regardless of the method used in securing the information. It provides a check to determine whether the job description statements are correct and if any task has been omitted. Assure each worker that any omitted responsibility that is recalled later will be included in the questionnaire.

Next, analyze carefully the duties listed on the several position questionnaires. Eliminate unnecessary duplication. Check for improper balance of duty assignments. For example, one or more of the higher paid office workers may be spending too much time on routine clerical duties. Another worker who is paid a lesser salary may be performing several tasks requiring greater clerical skills. In such instances, a reassignment of job duties may be necessary.

Writing Job Descriptions

In the process of distinguishing one job from another, two things are accomplished: all information is presented in a meaningful, accurate, and readable fashion, and the organization of statements on every position described is standardized so that all information can be compared easily and quickly.

The following steps are suggested for preparing a job description using the information on the job questionnaire:

• Summarize the duties and responsibilities of each position. Organize data appearing on the job questionnaire into proper relationships. For example, a job questionnaire may include the following separate statements:

> File alphabetically all correspondence
> Maintain a 4 by 6 visitation prospect file
> Maintain a record of prospects visited
> Maintain a card index file of members of the educational organizations

Other statements may refer to files, records, or schedules. To include each separate item in a job description summary would be cumbersome. The organization of these four items into one statement may be:

Maintain office files, records, and schedules.

A sample job questionnaire which a church employee completed is shown in Exhibit X. The chairman of the personnel committee used the information in Exhibit X to prepare the completed job description as shown in Exhibit XI.

On Exhibit X the employee listed thirteen regular duties and six others. Note that the word "type" was used in statements 6, 7, 8, and 13. In the job description, these four statements were combined into the two statements as shown in paragraphs 1 and 2 of Exhibit XI. The thirteen statements on the questionnaire were rewritten and combined into six statements on the job description.

Since statement 13 on the questionnaire "take dictation" was not a required regular duty, it was placed under "other duties."

The information on the back side of the questionnaire (see Exhibit X) is important also to determine the depth of the job requirements. Question 6, "Does this job require assigning rou-

EXHIBIT X

POSITION QUESTIONNAIRE FORM*

____Church

Present Job Title Office Secretary Date June

Name of Supervisor Minister of Education Prepared by Mary Brown

1. PRINCIPAL FUNCTION:

   To be in charge of all church paper and other mailing lists; type cards, letters, etc.; and have charge of the duplicating room.

2. REGULAR DUTIES: (List the major duties that your job normally requires you to perform)

   (1) Cut stencils; duplicate, and mail out "Choir Notes" once a week.
   (2) Cut stencils, duplicate and mail post cards to various groups.
   (3) Make duplicate cards on all new church members for financial, pastor's secretaries.
   (4) Send letter requests to churches for new members (notice of reception).
   (5) Once a month send letters of recommendation to those who request letters from us.
   (6) Type two educational organization enrolment cards for all new members and file them.
   (7) Type an eight-point record card for all new members.
   (8) Type report cards for secretaries of the educational organizations.
   (9) Make addressograph plates for new church members. Make plates for all changes of address and other files where names occur. Pull plates of any church member drops.
   (10) Ink all new addressograph plates, fill out state paper additions, drops, and changes of address.
   (11) Make out three copies of visitation slips: one is to be given out on Thursday, one is to be mailed to the department director, and the original copy is to be kept on file. File is kept up to date.
   (12) Mail out church bulletins; perform miscellaneous duplicating work.
   (13) Take dictation and do miscellaneous typing.

3. OTHER DUTIES: (List the duties you perform that are not on a regular basis.)

   (1) Keep duplicating room in order.
   (2) Cut stencils and duplicate materials for educational organizations who request it.
   (3) Order needed materials for this office and duplicating room.
   (4) Stuff church bulletins with inserts monthly.
   (5) Complete quarterly record cards for educational organizations.
   (6) Help count the offerings once or twice a quarter.

*Original questionnaire as completed by a church employee

(Please complete reverse side)

EXHIBIT X

POSITION QUESTIONNAIRE FORM*

(Page 2)

The following questions are intended to clarify the special skills, knowledge, and experience required to fulfil the normal requirements of the job.

4. WHAT KIND OF OFFICE EQUIPMENT DO YOU USE?

(Machine or Equipment)	(Usedoccasionally, frequently, continuously)
Typewriter	frequently
Duplicating Machine	frequently
Addressograph	frequently

5. WHAT SKILLS DOES THIS JOB REQUIRE? (Such as typing, shorthand, proofreading, filing, etc.)

Typing, shorthand, filing

6. DOES THIS JOB REQUIRE

(1) Assigning routine work to others? no

(2) Giving direct supervision to others? ____________

List names of those directly supervised, if any ____________

7. WHAT DECISIONS DO YOU NORMALLY MAKE IN THIS POSITION WITHOUT GETTING APPROVAL?

(Nature of the Decision)	(Frequency of Occurrence)
ordering office supplies	semimonthly

8. WHAT CONTACTS DO YOU MAKE WITH PEOPLE OUTSIDE THE CHURCH?

(Printers, vendors, etc)

(People contacted)	(Frequency of Occurrence)
delivery boys	daily
mailman	daily
calling suppliers	semimonthly

9. ADDITIONAL COMMENTS (Which will help to describe your job completely)

10. PLEASE WRITE WHAT YOU CONSIDER IS THE MAIN PURPOSE OF YOUR JOB

*Original questionnaire as completed by a church employee

EXHIBIT XI

POSITION DESCRIPTION FORM*

____CHURCH

Job Title Clerk-typist Date July

Supervised by Minister of Education

Prepared by Personnel Committee Chairman

Principal Function:

Maintain files, mailing lists, and records; operate duplicating and addressograph machines; type copy.

Regular Duties:

1. Type and process Training Union enrolment cards, eight-point record cards, and secretaries' weekly report cards.
2. Type and process cards on all new church members; request and send church membership letters.
3. Operate the duplicating machine for all duplicating work; keep duplicating room and supplies in order; cut stencils.
4. Maintain current member addressograph plate file for church bulletin and state Baptist paper mailings; make addressograph plates.
5. Maintain visitation prospect file; type up and distribute visitation slips as directed.
6. Mail out weekly the church paper.

Other Duties:

1. Order duplicating supplies.
2. Stuff envelopes for mailings.
3. Type copy and reports as assigned.
4. May take and transcribe dictation.
5. Assist as assigned.

Skills and other requirements:

1. Typing, shorthand, and filing.
2. High School Education.
3. Experience: helpful but not required.

*Job description prepared from information questionnaire in Exhibit 10.

tine work to others or giving direct supervision to others?" often reveals a misunderstanding of the organizational structure. An employee, who really has no supervisory responsibilities, may list the names of one or more workers whom she believes she supervises.

• Summarize skills and other requirements necessary for each job. Note that the job description form in Exhibit XI includes a space for listing skills and other requirements. If a job requires taking and transcribing dictation, decide the minimum typing and shorthand speeds acceptable. Establishing minimum skill and other job requirements are extremely important.

• Use language that is terse, direct, and specific.

Avoid using general terms such as "handle," "responsible for," or words like "seldom," "occasional," or "frequent." For example, it is difficult to know just what is meant by the statement "handle the mail." Another example of a general statement is "assemble copy for the church bulletin." The word "assemble" is not clear. It may mean "gather copy," or "edit copy," or "type copy," or a combination of two or more of these tasks.

It is essential then that the wording convey one definite meaning and not several possible meanings. The verbs should refer to specific action. For example, use verbs such as "operate," "type," "maintain," "requisition," "compile," "file," "enlist," "compose," "supervise." See the action verbs used in the sample job descriptions near the end of this chapter.

The present tense should be used throughout the job description. There should be a minimum of complicated sentence structure.

It is important that job descriptions be prepared accurately since they serve as the basis for determining the salary which the church will pay for each job.

Regardless of whether a staff supervisor writes the final position description or members of the personnel committee assist him, the finished description should be checked with the worker for clarity and completeness before the description is officially issued. Especially are discussions with workers necessary if tasks have been added, deleted, changed, or reassigned among the several employees. The arguments—to attain smoother work flow, to provide for a better balanced work load, to increase efficiency—may or may not be wholeheartedly accepted by all the workers. Their acceptance of change depends not only upon how well you kept them informed during the process of writing job descriptions but also upon your consideration in asking for their suggestions and ideas.

Several sample job descriptions are shown on pages 60–69. These are guides only. Every church should prepare its own descriptions to fit actual duties performed by the workers.

Maintaining and Using the Approved Job Descriptions

Since jobs change, all descriptions should be reviewed annually at least. The personnel committee may be assigned this responsibility. When the jobs change and the changes are approved, the descriptions involved may require rewriting.

The job descriptions along with the supporting job questionnaire data should be kept either in the pastor's office or in the office of another worker whom the pastor may designate. Copies may be maintained in both offices.

Each staff member should receive a typed copy of his approved job description. This is for the worker's personal use in checking the areas of his work responsibilities.

Whenever an additional staff member is needed, the new job should always be described before the person is placed on the payroll. This may mean a shift of responsibilities among several workers. The new job may fit the description of one already described. If not, a new job description and salary scale should be established.

Job descriptions not only help the church and the staff workers by defining jobs, but they also provide basic information for promoting harmonious staff worker-church relationships in the following areas:

- They serve as a guide for intelligent interviewing and placement. A person being interviewed for a staff vacancy should be

POSITION DESCRIPTIONS (Samples)

PASTOR

PRINCIPAL FUNCTION:

The pastor is responsible to the __________________________ Church for leading members to witness; to grow and develop in Christian maturity; and to participate in Christian ministries; and for acting as the administrator of the paid staff.

RESPONSIBILITIES:

1. Plan and conduct the worship services; prepare and deliver sermons; lead in observance of ordinances.

2. Visit members and prospects.

3. Conduct counseling sessions; perform wedding ceremonies; conduct funerals.

4. Serve as chairman of the church council to lead in planning, coordinating, and evaluating the total program of the church.

5. Work with deacons, church officers, and committees as they perform their assigned responsibilities.

6. Act as moderator of church business meetings.

7. Cooperate with associational, state, and denominational leaders in matters of mutual interest and concern; keep the church informed of denominational development; represent the church in civic matters.

8. Serve as administrator of the paid church staff; supervise the work of assigned paid staff workers.

CHURCH BUSINESS ADMINISTRATOR*

PRINCIPAL FUNCTION:

The church business administrator is responsible to the pastor for administering the business affairs of the church.

RESPONSIBILITIES:

1. Work with paid staff and church members to achieve the objectives of the church.

2. Establish and operate an efficient plan of financial record keeping and reporting; develop bookkeeping procedures.

3. Prepare financial information for the finance and budget committees and treasurer of the church.

4. Serve as resource person regarding legal and business matters of the church; study annually the insurance program in co-operation with the insurance committee.

5. Maintain records on church staff personnel; establish and maintain records on equipment and facilities.

6. Administer church adopted policies and procedures concerning the use of all church properties and facilities.

7. Assist church building committee in its relationships with architect, contractors, and others in building, remodeling, and equipping church buildings.

8. Serve on the church counsel; serve as exofficio member of the deacons and church committees.

9. Supervise workers in the maintenance and repair of all physical properties; establish and implement cleaning, painting, renovating schedules; operate within approved budget.

10. Supervise the operation of food services.

11. Supervise assigned office personnel.

*Several of the duties are usually included in the minister of education's position description when the church does not have a church business administrator.

MINISTER OF EDUCATION

PRINCIPAL FUNCTION:

The minister of education is responsible to the pastor for the development and promotion of the educational program of the church.

RESPONSIBILITIES:

1. Direct the planning, conducting, coordinating, and evaluating of a comprehensive education program based on program tasks.

2. Supervise the work of assigned paid staff workers.

3. Serve as a member of the church council.

4. Lead in enlisting and training organizational leadership in cooperation with the church nominating committee.

5. Organize and direct a churchwide visitation program.

6. Serve as a purchasing agent for the church as assigned; approve and process requisitions and purchase orders.

7. Maintain personnel records of all paid staff workers; execute church-approved personnel policies.

8. Develop projects such as youth camps, retreats, and appropriate activities for older constituents.

9. Edit church publications as assigned.

10. Assist the chairmen of the various church committees; serve as exofficio member of church committees.

11. Keep informed on methods, materials, principles, procedures, promotion, and administration as related to the education program.

12. Cooperate with association and state leaders in promoting activities of mutual interest.

MINISTER OF MUSIC

PRINCIPAL FUNCTION:

The minister of music is responsible to the pastor for the development and promotion of the music program of the church.

RESPONSIBILITIES:

1. Direct the planning, conducting, and evaluating of a comprehensive music program based on program tasks.

2. Supervise the work of assigned paid staff workers.

3. Cooperate with the church nominating committee to enlist and train leaders for the church Music Ministry, including graded choir workers, song leaders, and accompanists for the church organizations.

4. Lead in planning and promoting a graded choir program; direct and coordinate the work of lay choir workers; direct adult, youth, and junior choirs, and other choirs as needed.

5. Serve as a member of the church council; coordinate the music program with the organizational calendar and emphases of the church.

6. Lead the church to establish a music council; enlist and train members of the council; and guide the council in determining music objectives, goals, organization, leadership, facilities, finances, and administrative procedures

7. Assist the pastor in planning all services of worship.

8. Give direction to a Music Ministry plan of visitation.

9. Arrange and provide music for weddings, funerals, special projects, ministries, and other church-related activities upon request.

10. Maintain music library, materials, supplies, musical instruments and other equipment.

11. Keep informed on music methods, materials, promotion, and administration.

12. Cooperate with associational and state leaders in promoting activities of mutual interest.

Minister of Education and Music (Combination)

PRINCIPAL FUNCTION:

The Minister of Education and Music is responsible to the pastor for the development and promotion of the educational and music programs of the church.

RESPONSIBILITIES:

1. Direct the planning, coordinating, conducting, and evaluating of comprehensive educational and music programs based on program tasks.

2. Supervise the work of assigned paid staff members.

3. Serve as a member of the church council; lead the church to establish organizational councils; lead the church to enlist, train, and guide the councils in determining objectives, goals, organization, leadership, facilities, finances, and administrative procedures.

4. Lead in enlisting and training organizational leadership in cooperation with the church nominating committee.

5. Organize and direct a churchwide visitation program.

6. Assist the pastor in planning all services of worship; arrange and provide music for weddings, funeral, special projects, ministries and other church-related activities upon request.

7. Maintain personnel records of all paid staff workers; maintain music library, materials, supplies, musical instruments and other equipment.

8. Serve as the purchasing agent for the church as assigned.

9. Develop projects such as youth camps, retreats, and activities for older members.

10. Edit church publications as assigned.

11. Assist the chairmen of the various church committees; serve as ex officio member of church committees.

12. Keep informed on educational and music methods, materials, promotion and administration.

13. Cooperate with association and state leaders in promoting activities of mutual interest.

ORGANIST AND MUSIC ASSISTANT

PRINCIPAL FUNCTION:

The organist and music assistant is responsible to the minister of music for serving as organist of the church and assisting in the Music Ministry.

RESPONSIBILITIES:

1. Play for all services of the church, both regular and special.

2. Serve as accompanist for choirs, ensembles, and soloists in regular and special rehearsals and performances, as assigned.

3. Play for weddings and funerals, as requested, and with the approval of the minister of music.

4. Assist in planning worship services, choir rehearsals, and special music events.

5. Plan and give direction to a training program designed for developing organists and pianists in the church.

6. Maintain a regular schedule of organ practice and study.

7. Serve as secretary to the minister of music; take and transcribe dictation; and maintain Music Ministry files, library and equipment inventories.

8. Prepare workbooks and study materials for the graded choirs, as assigned.

9. Perform other related responsibilities, as assigned.

SECRETARY

PRINCIPAL FUNCTION:

Perform general office work in relieving supervisor of minor executive and clerical duties; take and transcribe dictation.

REGULAR DUTIES:

1. Take and transcribe dictation.

2. Perform general office work; maintain supplies and various files; keep records and compile these into periodic or occasional reports.

3. Review, open, digest, and distribute mail; prepare routine answers without direction, for approval and signature; answer routine letters in absence of the supervisor.

4. Act, as required, during supervisor's absence, in making decisions or taking any necessary action not requiring supervisory approval.

5. Exercise tact, courtesy, and diplomacy in receiving callers, personal or telephone; keep calendar of appointments.

6. Notify committee members of meeting dates.

OTHER DUTIES:

7. May edit and prepare bulletin copy for printer.

9. May order literature and office supplies.

10. May assist in training new office workers.

FINANCIAL SECRETARY

PRINCIPAL FUNCTION:

Maintain the church financial records and prepare financial reports periodically.

REGULAR DUTIES:

1. Receive, count, and deposit all church offerings.

2. Post receipts and disbursements of all accounts according to financial system.

3. Post offerings weekly to individual accounts; file envelopes.

4. Prepare bank reconciliation statements monthly.

5. Prepare financial reports for finance committee, deacons, and church business meetings; prepare and cut stencils for monthly and annual financial statements.

6. Prepare quarterly and annual government reports.

7. Check and total all invoices when approved; inform responsible persons of their budget expenditures.

8. Receive and answer queries concerning financial matters; maintain file of invoices, correspondence and reports.

9. Prepare and issue checks to staff members, designations, and organizations, in accordance with church policy.

10. Mail pledge cards, stewardship letters, and envelopes to new members.

OTHER DUTIES:

11. Requisition and prepare all forms and records for the annual stewardship emphasis.

12. Serve in related office duties, as assigned.

STENOGRAPHER

PRINCIPAL FUNCTION:

Take and transcribe dictation and perform general office work.

REGULAR DUTIES:

1. Take and transcribe dictation.

2. Perform general office work; maintain files and supplies; keep records, and compile these into periodic reports.

3. Type copy for reproduction.

4. Receive visitors; arrange appointments and keep calendar of appointments.

5. Receive and distribute incoming mail.

6. Answer the telephone.

OTHER DUTIES:

7. May assist in mailing out the bulletin.

8. Assist in clerical work as assigned.

CLERK-TYPIST

PRINCIPAL FUNCTION:

Maintain office files, records, and schedules; make requisitions, prepare reports, and type copy.

REGULAR DUTIES:

1. Maintain office files, records, and schedules.
2. Fill out requisition forms.
3. Prepare reports periodically, or as directed.
4. Do routine typing, and compose routine letters.
5. Correct addressograph mailing lists; operate addressograph.
6. Operate duplicating machine.

OTHER DUTIES:

7. May take and transcribe dictation.
8. May answer telephone and serve as receptionist.
9. Assist in clerical work as assigned.

TYPIST

PRINCIPAL FUNCTION:

Type routine copy; address envelopes.

REGULAR DUTIES:

1. Type routine form letters, copy, records, record cards, and reproduction masters.
2. Address and stuff envelopes.
3. Perform routine clerical work as assigned.

OTHER DUTIES:

4. May answer the telephone.
5. May sort and deliver incoming mail.
6. May maintain addressograph file.

CUSTODIAN

PRINCIPAL FUNCTION:

Maintain clean buildings and grounds.

REGULAR DUTIES:

1. Sweep, mop, buff, clean, and wax floors according to schedule; dust furniture and equipment; wash walls and windows, and vacuum carpets as scheduled.

2. Maintain clean restrooms; replenish tissue and towels; empty waste cans.

3. Request cleaning and maintenance supplies and equipment as needed.

4. Operate heating and cooling equipment according to schedule and instructions.

5. Prepare baptistry for use as directed and clean following use.

6. Open and close building daily as scheduled.

7. Mow grass; trim shrubbery, maintain clean church entrance, sidewalk, and parking areas.

8. Check with church office or supervisor daily for special assignments.

9. Move furniture, set up tables and chairs for suppers, banquets, and other similar occasions; and set up assembly and classroom areas for regular activities.

OTHER DUTIES:

10. Make minor electrical, plumbing, and equipment repairs as requested.

11. Paint walls, furniture, and equipment.

12. Perform messenger service.

13. Perform other duties as assigned.

told the duties of the job. A job description serves this purpose. In the selection process it helps in finding a person to fit the position rather than fitting the position to a person. A job description usually relieves any pressures to employ a person who is not qualified for the work.

In a church which has no written job descriptions, a newly employed person may be told in general terms what his tasks will be. In actual practice, this means that he must learn only through experience what his various and specific tasks are.

After accepting a job in a church, a new worker becomes disconcerted if he learns that not the half was told him regarding the major areas of his duties. Hardly a week may pass but that he is asked to do a task which was not mentioned in the initial interview.

To avoid such misunderstanding, it is very important to inform the new worker during the interview that, although the job includes definite areas of responsibilities which are named, he will be part of a team and may be asked occasionally to perform other tasks as the need may arise.

• They serve as a guide to the staff worker. It is difficult for a new worker to remember everything told him during the interview concerning the duties and responsibilities of his position. If he receives a copy of his job description, much of his frustration during the first few weeks as a new staff member can be eliminated and his confidence stimulated. The job description is his work guide. He checks himself against it. He talks to the pastor or to his supervisor if a statement of responsibility is not clear to him, or if he does not understand why he performs it.

• They identify workers by position title. The title of the position is determined by the job description statements. For example, a position that has, as a major duty, taking and transcribing dictation may be titled "stenographer" even though other duties, such as performing general office work, maintaining files and supplies, receiving visitors, distributing incoming mail, answering the telephone, may also be included.

But, suppose that the major areas of the position are to maintain office files, records, and schedules, do routine typing, operate the duplicating machine, and that taking and transcribing dictation is only a minor or infrequent duty. In this case, the job might be titled "office clerk" or "clerk-typist" even though both jobs include taking and transcribing dictation. This task in the first example is the principal duty of the job while in the second description it is a minor duty.

In a smaller church, the pastor may have only one person to assist him. The part-time worker may do all the office and clerical work. She may keep the church roll, take and transcribe dictation, answer the telephone, maintain financial records, and may be called upon to help enlist leadership for the educational organizations of the church. The titles "stenographer" or "financial secretary" obviously do not fit. A more descriptive job title would be either "office secretary" or "church secretary."

When the staff is increased from one to two workers, or more, churches sometimes fail to see the importance of identifying the new people as well as present workers by descriptive job titles. Job titles are based upon the content of the job. Obviously, every office worker should not be identified as "secretary." See Exhibit XII for a list of job titles frequently used in churches.

Exhibit XII
A List of Position Titles Used in Churches

Pastor	Educational Secretary
Associate Pastor	Office Secretary
Assistant to the Pastor	Financial Secretary
Senior Minister	Financial Clerk
Minister	Posting Clerk
Minister of Education	Stenographer
Minister of Music	Receptionist
Church Organist	Clerk-Typist
Church Business Administrator	Records Clerk
Director of Adult Work	Typist
Director of Youth Work	Office Clerk
Director of Children's Work	Maintenance Supervisor
Director of Recreation	Buildings and Grounds Superintendent
Church Visitor	Custodian

Church Hostess	Gardener
Pastor's Secretary	Janitor
Church Secretary	Maid
Music Secretary	Cook

• They reveal unnecessary work duplication. Every office has some work duplication. Some is necessary. Some is planned as the best way to perform the work efficiently. Generally, work duplication should be reduced or eliminated.

For example, in one church after a study of job questionnaires, two people in different offices were discovered to be maintaining the complete church roll. Originally, the roll was assigned to one person. However, the second worker who used the church roll only occasionally decided that she needed one also. Any task duplication that is not required for the efficient performance of a job, is a waste of time and money.

• They uncover improper balance of duty assignments. Sometimes a person's job comes gradually to include assignments that began as emergencies. Such assignments usually are given to the most cooperative individual on the staff without regard for his regular work. Eventually, these new duties become either a regular part of the position or dangling appendages. As a result, one or more of the highest paid office workers may be spending too much time in routine clerical duties. Conversely, one or more lesser paid workers may be performing highly skilled tasks.

Suppose an office worker in a large church accumulated the following responsibilities:

a Take and transcribe dictation
b Keep mailing lists up to date
c Operate the duplicating machine
d Type from copy
e Stuff and seal envelopes
f Mail the weekly church bulletin
g File correspondence

Obviously, duty *a* is out of place since the remaining six duties are routine. The six duties are necessary, but they can be performed by a worker who has no stenographic skills.

For another example, suppose a second worker in the same office accumulated through the years the following duties:

a Answer the telephone
b Keep bulletin boards cleared of old posters
c Type form letters
d Receive, open, and distribute mail
e Exercise tact, courtesy, and diplomacy in receiving visitors
f Take and transcribe dictation

Quite evidently, the second worker has two high level clerical responsibilities, *e* and *f*, mixed in with several routine duties. Whenever feasible, the more routine clerical responsibilities should be grouped into one job description and the higher level duties into another. In a smaller church office such groupings may be impractical. However, when a new clerical worker is added to the staff, the pastor or other supervisor should be alert to the feasibility of reassigning and regrouping the tasks among the several workers.

• They serve as a guide to study salaries of comparable positions in a community. Occasionally, churches may be able to employ individuals without regard to prevailing salaries for comparable jobs. Sooner or later, however, a church finds it necessary to increase salary schedules if it is to employ and hold workers qualified to perform the various jobs. To employ inexperienced or unqualified persons at lower rates to do high-level work is poor economy.

In order to make salary comparisons meaningful, church job descriptions must be comparable to those outside the church. For example, the job title "secretary" does not always refer to the same position in every church or business establishment. In one office, the clerk-typist may be called a secretary; in another, a stenographer may be so designated. It is impossible to make comparable salary studies in the community based only on position titles. Written job descriptions must be compared.

• They aid in measuring the job performance of the worker. To measure performance objectively involves more than a general, cursory estimate of a person's performance in his position.

The job description statements help the supervisor as he talks to a worker about his performance.

• They serve as a guide for promotion. An important factor in developing staff morale is the placement of a worker in a job which he can perform. As an individual develops, he may be eligible for a more highly rated position when a vacancy occurs. It is much better to promote a qualified person already on the church staff than to recruit a new worker from outside.

In a large church, a chain reaction may start when a vacancy occurs. For example, the pastor's secretary resigns. A stenographer, working in some other office in the church, is promoted to this position. A stenographic vacancy then exists. In the same office is a typist or clerk who is qualified for promotion to the stenographic job. Now a typist's position is vacant. This vacancy would probably be filled by a person from outside the office. Assuming that the people involved are promotable, the policy of promoting from within is a sound program of personnel administration. It develops good relations and usually reduces training costs.

• They aid in a smoother flow of work. Since job descriptions define specific work responsibilities, they help to discover and overcome work-flow bottlenecks. In one church, for example, job questionnaires revealed why church members did not always receive the weekly issue of the church paper by Friday. The individual in charge of typing, duplicating, and mailing was frequently delayed by the one in charge of gathering, editing, and compiling the copy. She, in turn, was delayed because it was most difficult to secure copy from the various church organization personnel earlier than Wednesday afternoon.

As a result, the pastor, with the help of the personnel committee, prepared a revised work-flow procedure and sent a copy to everyone involved.

• They help develop staff morale. Job descriptions are an indication to staff members of the church's interest in them and their work. The first step toward good work organization and coordination is the writing of job descriptions. The worker feels that he is part of a team. He knows what is expected of him. Job descriptions serve as a definition of the church's expectations.

• They make for effective control of job content. A supervisor, who believes that he knows every detail of the work performed by those under his supervision, is surprised when he learns that a certain job is different from that originally assigned or described.

For example, in one church the financial secretary remarked to her supervisor on several occasions that it was impossible to complete her work each day. Occasionally, she worked at nights and on Saturdays in order to maintain the records and compile reports, so the church employed a half-time clerical worker to assist her. Later, a job questionnaire revealed that for several months the financial secretary had been keeping separate bookkeeping records for one of the church educational organizations. This was not part of her assigned job. Somehow, the additional responsibility had been placed on her desk without the supervisor's knowledge.

In another church, a janitor was asked by the various church workers to run so many errands that getting his own work done became impossible. The situation continued for several months. When it was discovered, the janitor was reluctant to return to his old job stating that he was now a church messenger.

Workers in a church are usually vulnerable to the work requests, even demands, of church leaders. To control this situation it is wise to channel all requests to a specific worker: the minister of education, church business administrator, educational secretary, or some other designated person.

• They form a basis for setting up a formalized salary program. A principal reason for preparing job descriptions is to evaluate the relative worth of various jobs in order to assign dollar value to each. See chapter 5 for information on setting up a church salary program.

• They are an aid in preparing the church staff organization chart. An organization chart shows the names of all paid staff workers, their job titles, their peer and supervisory relationships.

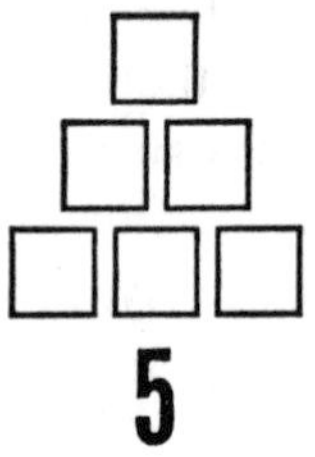

5

Paying the Worker What the Job Is Worth

Is it better to have staff workers speculating among themselves whether salary increases will be recommended in next year's budget or for the church to have a written salary plan?

Generally, workers feel more secure in their jobs and evidence less frustration when they know that the church has a salary plan that carries over from year to year. A formalized salary plan has several advantages:

• A budget, or finance, committee is not placed in the difficult position of making decisions apart from a church-approved salary plan. One question invariably asked by the committee members is: what, if anything, should we do about salary increases next year for the staff workers?

The resultant salary adjustment is usually a blanket increase with little or no regard for individual job performance. Sometimes, the committee feels that one of the workers does not deserve a salary adjustment, and increases are withheld from all workers. Occasionally, varying amounts of salary increases are decided, seemingly, without rhyme or reason.

A formalized salary plan provides a committee with detailed salary increase information to cover the next year's salary needs.

• No worker is overlooked for salary review. A formalized

salary plan includes setting up a salary review file card on each worker who is in the plan. The file card shows the worker's employment date from which the salary review dates are determined. The possibility of bypassing a review date then becomes remote.

• All workers are treated fairly. A salary plan eliminates the possibility of one or more workers receiving a salary adjustment shortly after they are placed on the payroll or having to wait longer than twelve months.

For example, suppose a church employs worker A in October and, as is its custom, salary adjustments are always effective in January. Suppose further that worker B was employed the previous February. Assuming that both workers were employed at the same base salary, chances are that without a salary plan both workers, A and B, will, on January 1, receive increases: one after three months on the job and the other after eleven months. Would worker B, employed in February, feel that he was treated fairly? Of course not.

Suppose that the committee, in this example, decides not to give worker A who came to the staff in October an increase because of the shortness of his tenure. This decision seems reasonable. However, the next salary adjustment consideration by the committee will be a year hence. Worker A, then, may wait fifteen months for a salary increase. Would worker A feel that he had been treated fairly? Obviously not.

The success of any salary program depends upon how consistently the plan is administered from year to year.

Any church, large or small, can establish an acceptable and workable salary program. The personnel committee is the logical one to assist the pastor and other staff supervisors to establish a salary program.

For purposes of this presentation, the salaries of the office and maintenance workers are primarily considered, although the pastor, minister of education, church business administrator, minister of music, recreation director, age-group directors, and others may be included in a formalized salary plan. Generally, the same principles of salary administration apply to all workers on a church staff.

Setting Up a Salary Program

Here are several of the steps that may be followed in setting up a salary program:

Prepare written descriptions.—See chapter 4 for suggestions for preparing written job or position descriptions.

Rate the jobs.—Descriptions form a basis for determining the relative worth of the several jobs. Keep in mind that *jobs* are rated as to salary worth, *not the workers* who hold the jobs.

Use the ranking method described below to rate the jobs. It is a simple method of interrelating thirty-five, or fewer, different job descriptions. To get the most objective ratings, do not place the names of the workers on the written job descriptions.

To rank the descriptions, select the position description that requires the most skill and ability for successful performance and place it on top of the stack. Next, select the description that requires the least skill and ability and place it on the bottom of the stack. Then, rank the other descriptions between these two. Two or more jobs may rank the same, even though the duties are different.

Suppose there are six different job descriptions to be rated. They are identified as jobs A, B, C, D, E, and F. Suppose further, that members of the personnel (or other) committee are to rank the positions. At the rating session give each member a complete set of the six descriptions. Instruct them in the ranking method. Read and explain the jobs.

After all members of the committee finish ranking the six jobs, discuss the results to reach agreement. One method of helping the group reach a consensus is to draw a chart on the chalkboard, placing the names of the ranking team down the left side and the job names across the top. Then draw in the horizontal and vertical lines. See Exhibit XIII.

Ask every member to rank each job while another writes the ratings in the proper boxes on the chart. Agree ahead of time that

Exhibit XIII

Chart Showing Individual and Team Ranking of Each of the Six Jobs

Ranking Team	*Job Titles*					
	A	B	C	D	E	F
Henry	3	4	1	6	5	2
Carl	3	5	2	6	4	1
Walter	2	5	1	6	4	3
Harvey	3	5	1	6	4	2
Bill	2	5	1	6	4	3
Pastor	2	5	1	6	4	3
Total	15	29	7	36	25	14
Team Ranking	2.5	4.9	1.2	6.0	4.1	2.3

no one will comment until the exercise is completed. See Exhibit XIII for a sample of the job rankings for the six descriptions.

Compare the rankings. In the example everyone agrees that job D ranks sixth, and five members agree that job C ranks first. The next step is to reach agreement as to the rankings of the remaining four jobs. Now, give members an opportunity to ask one another questions about variances in their rankings. Hopefully, the discussion will lead to a consensus.

During the discussion someone may ask for the names of the actual workers in the various jobs. As tactfully as possible, explain that the workers will be identified later when the job ranking is completed.

Another way to reach general agreement is to total the committee's rankings of each job. See Exhibit XIII. Then divide the total by six to arrive at the team ranking for each job. Usually this exercise reveals rather clearly group concensus. In the illustration in Exhibit XIII the committee arrived at the following rankings:

Job	*Ranking*
C	1
F	2
A	3
E	4
B	5
D	6

It is possible that the group may agree to rate jobs A and F equal since they rank close together in total average points.

Determine the starting salary.—What salaries should a church pay for the various jobs? Probably it will want salaries to be comparable to those paid in the community for similarly described jobs. There are several ways to get salary information.

One way is to ask other pastors, ministers of education, or business administrators in the city what salaries their churches pay for comparable jobs. Always be willing to reciprocate salary information.

Certain other sources are usually available. A member of the church, who is a personnel officer in a local business establishment, is usually willing to cooperate. One could check with several businessmen in the church or in the community to determine if a local business firm or a trade association makes an annual salary survey. A local salary survey compiled within the past twelve months is one of the best sources of information on ranges and average rates paid in the community.

Suppose the community monthly rate for job C ranges from $300 to $450 with an average salary of $375; for job E from $250 to $375 with an average salary of $300; and for job D from $190 to $275 with an average of 230. (These are hypothetical salaries.)

With these facts, the members of the personnel committee are ready to establish starting rates for these three jobs. Determine first if the church wishes to pay the average rates in the community as the starting rates for the church jobs, or some dollar figure between the bottom of the range and the average rate for each job. Generally, the latter suggestion is more appropriate since it places the starting rates slightly below the average in the community but in a good competitive position. Suppose the latter policy is acceptable. The starting salaries for three of the six jobs would be as follows:

Job	*Rank*	*Starting Salary*
C	1	$350
F	2	
A	3	
E	4	275
B	5	
D	6	215

The next step is to determine the starting salary of the remaining three jobs: F, A, and B. Suppose, in this example, that the committee decides that the total points of jobs F and A are close enough to justify the same starting salary. The established starting salaries for all six jobs might appear as follows:

Job	*Rank*	*Starting Salary*
C	1	$350
F	2–3	325
A	2–3	325
E	4	275
B	5	250
D	6	215

Since job C rates $350 and ranks *1*, and job E rates $275 and ranks *4*, establish the rates for jobs F and A (which rank between jobs C and E) below $350 but above $275. Job B is rated similarly between the established salaries of jobs D and E.

Determine the maximum salary.—After the starting salaries are determined, the next step is to decide the maximum salary for each job.

The salary spread between the minimum (starting) and the maximum (top) salary for each job is usually based upon an agreed percentage. The same percentage is applied to the starting salary of each job included in the study. The percentages used in business generally range from 20 to 40. The pastor and the committee may decide on 20, 25, 30, 33⅓, 40 or some other percent. Suppose the committee selected 25 percent as the desired range between the starting and top salary for each job. The salary spread for the six sample jobs would be as follows:

Job	*Starting Salary*	*Maximum Salary*	*Salary Spread*
C	$350	$438	$88
F	325	406	81
A	325	406	81
E	275	344	69
B	250	313	63
D	215	269	54

Twenty-five percent of $350 (job C) is $88. This figure represents the amount of money—the spread—between the starting rate and the maximum rate of job C. Apply the same percentage to arrive at the dollar spread for the other five jobs.

Determine the amount of step increase.—The next step in setting up a salary program is for the pastor and the committee to determine how much of the salary spread is a fair salary step increase for each job.

One impartial method is to fix a definite percentage of each job's salary spread to apply to all jobs in the study. Suppose 20 percent of the spread is selected for a step increase. Twenty percent of the spread of job C ($88) is a $17 increase for Steps two and three and an $18 increase each for Steps four, five, and six. When $88.00 is divided by five (20 percent), the result is $17.00 with $3.00 remaining. It is added at $1.00 each to Steps four, five, and six making the value of these steps $18.00.

The complete salary scale for job C is as follows:

Step 1 (starting salary)	$350
Step 2 ($350 plus $17)	367
Step 3 ($367 plus $17)	384
Step 4 ($384 plus $18)	402
Step 5 ($402 plus $18)	420
Step 6 ($420 plus $18)	438 (maximum salary)

The step increases of the other five jobs in the example are figured in the same way. The complete salary schedule of the six jobs is shown in Exhibit XIV.

Exhibit XIV

Chart Showing Dollar Step Values of Job Titles

Steps	*Job Titles* D	B	E	A	F	C
1	$215	$250	$275	$325	$325	$350
2	225	262	288	341	341	367
3	236	274	302	357	357	384
4	247	287	316	373	373	402
5	258	300	330	389	389	420
6	269	313	344	406	406	438

Next, prepare a graph showing the dollar value of each job's salary steps. On the left-hand side of the graph write in the dollar scale. On the bottom of the graph write in the job titles. The next step is to pinpoint on the graph the base and maximum rates of each job. Now draw a short horizontal line (one-half inch or so) through each of the minimum and maximum points. Then connect each set of horizontal lines with vertical lines. The rectangular shaped figure is called a pay grade. To complete each pay grade draw in the four horizontal lines within each pay grade to coincide with the step increase values. See Exhibit XV.

A salary graph shows the dollar-value relationships between steps as well as between pay grades. Also, the amount of overlap between one pay grade and the next one higher or lower, is readily seen.

Salary charts and graphs should not be distributed to the workers.

Determine salary review dates.—How often should the salaries of workers be reviewed? every six months? every twelve months? some other plan? The pastor and the committee must make the decision. A common practice is to review the salary of a new worker after six months of continuous employment and annually thereafter. Some business firms review salaries of clerical and maintenance workers more often during the first two

EXHIBIT XV

GRAPH SHOWING JOB TITLES, PAY GRADES, AND DOLLAR VALUE OF EACH STEP

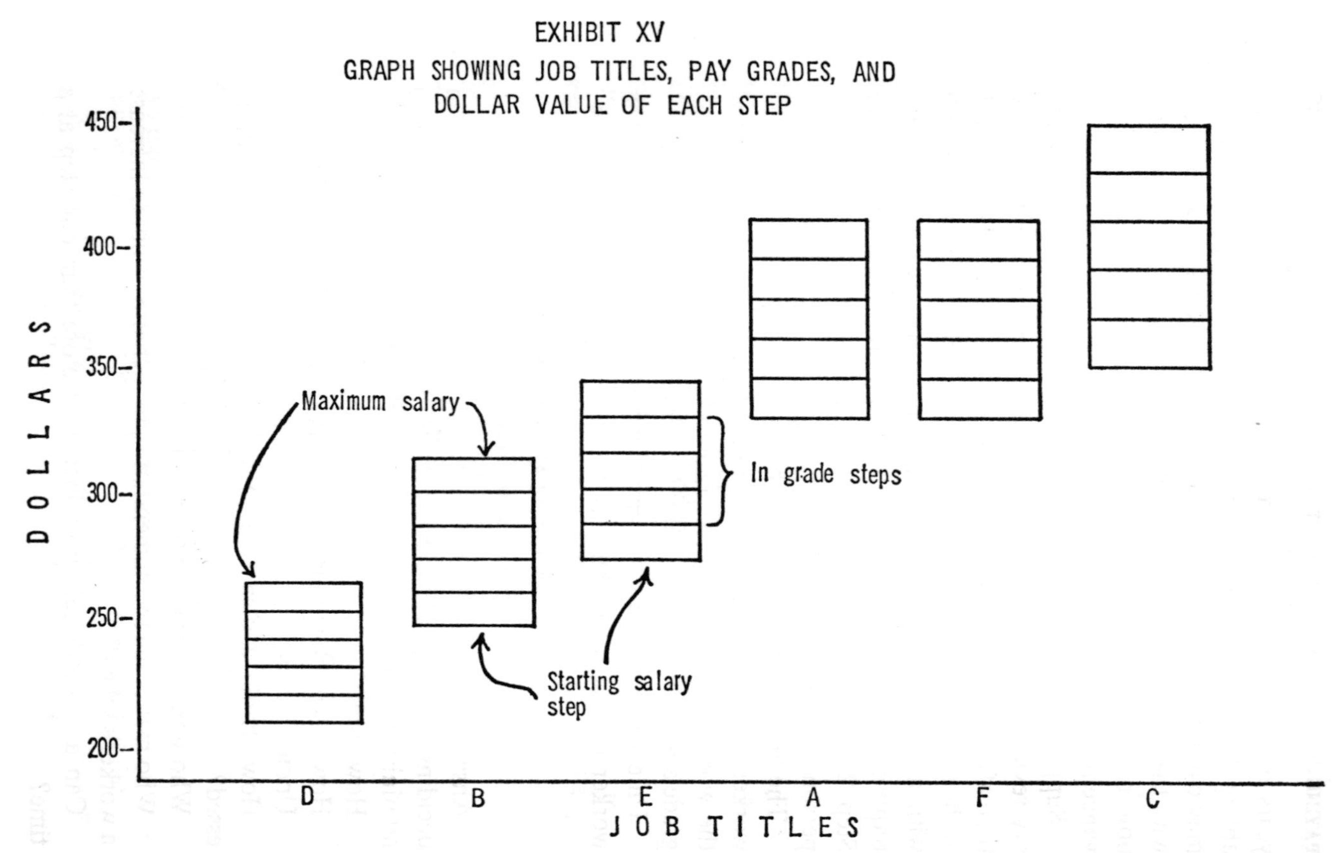

years of employment. However, a shortened time schedule enabling the workers to climb the salary ladder in two years or so may cause serious personnel problems. For example: what to do with the employee who has reached the top of his pay grade and now complains he has no further opportunities for salary advancement.

Suppose the pastor and the committee mutually agree on salary review dates of six months for new employees and annually thereafter. If a new worker is employed on job E on December 1 at the starting salary rate of $275, he is eligible in June for Step 2 with a salary of $288, provided that he has met performance requirements. The month of June, when the worker has attained Step 2, is set up as the annual salary review month for this person.

The term often used to describe the annual review date of each worker is "pay grade anniversary month." Therefore, unless the worker on job E is promoted to a higher paid job, his pay grade anniversary month is fixed as June.

Unless two workers are employed in the same month, each worker on the paid staff has a different salary review month.

Deciding Policy and Procedure Statements

Answers to the following questions will serve as guides in deciding what policy and procedure statements are needed to administer a salary program.

How often should salaries of workers be reviewed?

How should pay grade anniversary dates be established?

Upon what basis shall a worker's salary be increased?

How should a demotion, transfer, or a promotion be processed?

Who starts the salary review action?

Who makes the recommendation to increase or not to increase a worker's salary?

Can a worker's salary be increased more than one step at a time?

Who gives the final approval of the salary increase recommendations?

Who informs the worker of the action taken?

Shall a new worker always start at step one of his salary grade or will experience or other consideration affect his starting salary?

Shall a person ever receive more than the maximum salary step for his pay grade? If so, on what basis? tenure of service? performance? both?

How often should job descriptions be reviewed?

How often should church salary scales be compared with the community rates?

Who shall maintain the salary policies and procedures manual?

How often shall the salary policies and procedures be reviewed? Who will do it?

The written policies and procedures of each church will answer these or similar questions. See Exhibits XX and XXI for information on sample policy and procedure formats. Perhaps written policies and procedures covering vacations, holidays, work hours, time off with or without pay, group insurance, retirement, and others have already been prepared. A formalized salary administration manual includes documents similarly prepared.

On the question "How process a demotion, transfer, or a promotion," the committee may come to these conclusions:

• Demotions. Suppose a worker is in job E at Step 3 which is $302 a month (See Exhibit XIV). Because of lack of ability or other similar reason, she is demoted to job B. It may be desirable to write into policy that a demoted worker's salary shall be adjusted to the same step number in the lower pay grade as in the higher pay grade at the time of demotion. In this example, the worker's salary would be reduced from $302 to $274 a month. Or there could be included a policy statement indicating that the demoted worker's salary shall be adjusted to the nearest comparable rate in the lower pay grade. Again, in this example, the worker's salary would be reduced from $302 (Step 3) to $300 (Step 5 of job B) a month.

The latter policy has two inherent problems: (1) The supposedly demoted worker continues to receive a comparable salary for a lower rated job; and (2) "jumping" his salary from Step 3 to Step 5 gives him very little opportunity for salary advancement.

• Transfers. Usually, a transfer places a worker in another job with the same pay scale. For example, suppose a worker is in job A at Step 4 which is $373 a month. If he is transferred to job F, he would make a lateral move and remain at Step 4 salary in the new job. Or the church may wish to write another transfer plan into its policy statement.

• Promotions. Usually a promotion means moving a worker to a higher rated job and with an increase in salary. Look again at Exhibit XIV. Suppose a worker in job E at Step 4 salary of $316 is promoted to job A. To what salary step in job A should he be promoted? The committee needs to make the decision in the form of a policy statement which will guide it in this and future actions.

If the promoted worker is to be placed in a salary step equal to or next higher than he is presently receiving, his salary could be adjusted from $316 (Step 4 in pay grade of job E) to $325 (Step 1 in pay grade of job A). This is a monthly increase of $9.00. However, the total step increase for job A is $16 (the difference between $325, Step 1, and $341, Step 2). This means that the promoted worker lacked $7.00 receiving a full step increase.

This problem could be resolved in several ways.

One is to agree that $7 (in this example) is ample and appropriate and to assume that the salary matter will be corrected at his next pay grade anniversary date. But suppose the increase was only $1 or that his pay grade anniversary date was eleven months away or that his promotion coincided with his pay grade anniversary date?

Another way is to assign the promoted worker a new pay

grade anniversary month. His new anniversary date may be figured by using the following formula:

$$\frac{9 \text{ (actual increase)}}{16 \text{ (total step increase)}} \text{ times } \frac{6 \text{(six months)}}{1}$$

$$\text{equals } \frac{54}{16} \text{ or } 3 \text{ (3 months)}$$

His new salary anniversary date is set up for three months hence of the month of actual promotion instead of the usual six months (Step 1 to Step 2 time elapse). In this example it is assumed that the policy is to promote a worker from Step 1 to Step 2 after six month's employment. Substitute the number *12* (12 months) in the formula to figure the pay grade anniversary date of a worker who is promoted to Step 2 or above in a higher pay grade.

Or, rather than follow the formula method, the church may wish to have written into policy that, whenever a worker's increase is less than a full step increase in the higher pay grade, his new anniversary date will automatically be set up six months in advance.

Yet another method is to promote the worker to the salary step in the higher pay grade which includes at least a full step increase. In this example, then, the worker's salary would move from $316 (Step 4) to $341 (Step 2) a month which is $10 more than the normal step increase for that pay grade. His pay grade anniversary date would be changed to agree with the month of actual promotion.

A policy is written to be lived by. Do not make exceptions. If a policy or a procedure is found to be no longer applicable or workable, rewrite it. Review the policies and procedures manual annually.

Carrying Out the Salary Program

Secure church approval.—Prepare a written recommendation outlining the salary program. Include sample salary schedules and distribute them to the church members in a business meeting. They will then know what is being considered when the report is presented for their approval. Answer questions directly and clearly.

Some important steps.—Set up a salary record on each worker. The record should include information such as name, address, employment date, job title, present salary, dates of salary increases, name of supervisor. Provide additional spaces for entries related to promotion, transfer, or other changes in salary status.

When the salary program is implemented, some of the workers' salaries may not coincide with any salary step in the new scale. Suppose that the worker who holds the position of job E (See Exhibit XIV) presently receives $280 a month. The new scale provides salary steps of $275, $288, $302 a month. The worker can be paid at $280 (his present salary) until the month of his employment anniversary and then his salary can be adjusted to $288. Or his salary can be increased to $288 immediately, and his new anniversary date can be refigured according to the formula above or by some other method. A consistent course of action needs to be determined.

Usually, the salary of a worker which is below Step 1 of a new salary program is brought to Step 1 immediately. The salary of a worker that is more than the top step of his salary scale remains unchanged (frozen) until such time as the economy moves upward or a job promotion is effected. Whatever action is decided it must be applied alike to all workers included in the salary study.

An important step in implementing a salary program is to discuss the new or revised salary policies and procedures with the workers. Explain the purpose of a formalized salary program. They are entitled to know about church actions that affect them. Discuss privately with each worker how the new or revised salary scale will affect his salary. The supervisor is the logical person to do this with the workers whom he supervises.

Another important aspect of a good salary program is maintenance. The plan must be consistently administered from year to year. A formalized plan, therefore, is essential.

Budget the salaries.—A formalized salary plan takes the guesswork out of budgeting pay increases. The supervisor knows:

Every job's pay scale
Every worker's salary step
Every worker's pay grade anniversary date

With these three facts, he can prepare for the budget or finance committee a report showing the total amount of pay increase and salary to be budgeted for each worker during the coming year.

Suppose six workers are in jobs D, B, E, A, F, and C and each worker has a different pay grade anniversary date. To prepare salary information for the budget committee, a salary increase schedule may be prepared as shown in Exhibit XVI. For purposes of this example, January is the beginning date of the budget year.

The schedule shows that $576 is the total possible amount of annual salary increase to be budgeted for the six workers. This amount, of course, is in addition to the $1871 monthly or $22,452 annual salary cost presently paid these six workers.

This example of salary budgeting assumes that no terminations will occur during the next twelve months and that every worker will receive his increase—assumptions which may or may not be valid.

For example, it is possible that the worker in job B may terminate in March of next year. If so, the replacement's salary is $250 (Step 1) a month for six months and then $262 (Step 2) for the remaining months of that year. It is also possible that the worker in job A, when reviewed on job performance, may not receive an increase to Step 5 in June. The amount of the budgeted salary increase, $112, remains unexpended.

For budgeting purposes, a program of salary administration has another advantage. The pastor or the personnel committee is able to plan ahead for any needed expansion of staff workers. When a new job is approved, the base salary determined, and the month agreed upon for employment of the worker, the pastor, or

Exhibit XVI

Chart Showing Cost of Employee Salary Increases for the Next Budget Year

Name	*Job Title*	*Present Monthly Salary*	*Present Step*	*Next Step Salary*	*Amount of Increase*	*Paygrade Anniv. Date*	*Number of Months*	*Total Monthly Increase*
Brooks	D	225.00	2	236.00	11.00	February	11	121.00
Case	B	274.00	3	287.00	13.00	November	2	26.00
Smith	E	275.00	1	288.00	13.00	January	12	156.00
Jones	A	373.00	4	389.00	16.00	June	7	112.00
Hammond	F	357.00	3	373.00	16.00	April	9	144.00
Steele	C	367.00	2	384.00	17.00	December	1	17.00
Totals		$1871.00						$576.00

the personnel committee, is prepared to give accurate salary information to the budget committee.

Keep the salary program simple. A complicated plan discourages maintenance. Once a plan is established, work it; abide by it. A consistent year-by-year administration of a salary plan is an absolute necessity as a support for building a staff into a team.

Strange as it may seem, once employees work under a well-administered formalized salary plan and experience its advantages, they are enthusiastic in their support of it and would be most reluctant to return to the "good old days."

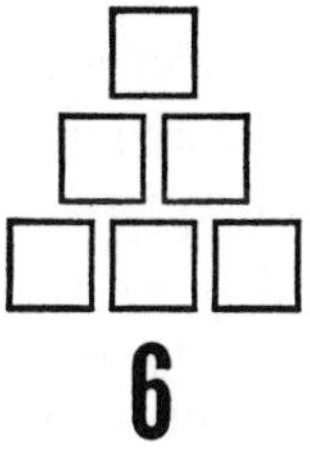

6

Helping the Worker Develop on the Job

Almost everyone wants to know how he is progressing and will accept suggestions for improving his work. He looks to his supervisor to help him get ahead. Lawrence A. Appley, President, American Management Association, writes:

> Surveys have shown that one of the desires most commonly expressed by employees is for more complete and accurate information on "How Am I Doing." Each employee wants a clear knowledge of what he is expected to do, how well he is expected to do it, how well he is doing it, how he might do it better, and how he might qualify for greater responsibilities.
>
> If the extent to which individuals are kept informed of their progress, and the skill with which this is done, were to be tripled in every organization in the next twelve months, the resulting impact upon company performance, our economy, and society in general would be almost beyond comprehension. Frustrations, complexes, misunderstandings are all fed by our neglecting to deal personally and individually with those who look to us for leadership.
>
> This means that managers must have strong personal relationships with their people so that they can discuss all these things frankly, openly and fairly. This, plus the skill to motivate, is the power of leadership.[1]

[1] *How Am I Doing Talks* (Personnel Administration Department, General Mills, Inc., Minneapolis, Minn.), p. 1.

It is generally agreed that nothing is more important or will accomplish more in the motivation and development of workers than for the most immediate supervisor to plan and conduct regularly scheduled employee development appraisal interviews with his workers.

The Employee Development Appraisal

Appraisal is an attempt by the supervisor to think clearly about each worker's job performance and how he can help the worker improve it. The main purpose of an appraisal plan is to help each worker do a better job in his present position.

Day-to-day coaching is important but does not meet the total needs of a worker as do regularly scheduled "how am I doing" talks. These talks help an employee get greater satisfaction from his work and do a better job. Appraisals are intended to help the supervisor and worker understand each other better, to review the worker's problems, to elicit his ideas, and to decide how a more successful supervisor-worker team can be achieved.

Uses of the appraisal.—The uses of appraisal may be grouped into two main areas:

- Salary increases
- Improvement and development of workers.

Decide first the purpose of the appraisal plan. Is it to help in determining if workers merit salary increases? Or is it to give guidance in helping the worker to improve and develop on his job? The same appraisal form cannot adequately serve both uses.

Generally, experience has proved that an appraisal plan designed to serve both of the above uses fails to motivate employees to a program of self-development. Workers feel inhibited when they know that the purpose of an appraisal interview is a mixture of work improvement talk and an effort on the supervisor's part to decide whether to approve a salary increase. It is practically impossible to divorce the process of an appraisal interview from its intended consequences.

An appraisal plan, therefore, cannot serve "two masters." A supervisor learns much about workers in appraisal interviews that helps to guide him in future decisions about them. Salary and job promotion decisions should be based upon the best information available. The day-to-day coaching plus employee development appraisal interviews give the supervisor a vast store of knowledge about each worker. One mark of a good supervisor is his ability to sift all the information he has learned about his workers and, excluding personal biases and prejudices, make appropriate decisions affecting every aspect of their work life.

The plan suggested below is based on the use of appraisal interviews for improvement and development of workers. See Exhibit XVII for a suggested employee development appraisal form.

The Appraiser.—The most immediate supervisor is the best qualified to appraise. He represents an accountability center. He is responsible for work production. The quantity and quality of production is directly related to the general morale of the workers—how they feel about themselves and others in a team relationship.

The supervisor makes judgments of worker effectiveness. If these are snap judgments and are made without formal appraisals, they could become the basis for decisions that seriously affect the worker as well as the work. An appraisal plan reduces impulsive judgments. Instead, through mutual interaction and discussion, opinions which are shared by supervisor and worker form the basis for corrective action and employee development.

Some church staff supervisors have the notion that since all the workers are Christian they automatically have a camaraderie that is mutually supportive. This may be only in the supervisor's mind. The workers, on the other hand, may hopefully long for the day when their supervisor would just discuss with them some of the things they have on their minds.

Other supervisors have a paternalistic or autocratic attitude toward their workers. They give orders and expect them to be obeyed without much regard for the worker's feelings. In this work climate the feelings of the employees may be similar to that of a ten-year-old boy who was traveling with his parents. One

EXHIBIT XVII

EMPLOYEE DEVELOPMENT INTERVIEW

Name of Supervisor______________________________Date__________________

Name of Employee____

The purpose of this interview is fourfold:

1. The supervisor and the employee review the employee's job description for accuracy and completeness and to discuss areas of needed improvement;

2. The supervisor and the employee agree on the job skills required in the worker's job. Skills may be such things as planning, organizing, writing, preparing talks, conducting conferences, evaluating program results, typing, posting, filing, receptionist work.

3. The supervisor and the employee discuss the employee's job performance based on these job skills.

4. The supervisor and employee agree on an improvement plan for the employee to match his job skill needs.

EMPLOYEE COMPLETES THIS SECTION

1. List the skills required by your job description.

2. In which skills do you feel you have done your best work?

3. In which skills do you feel you need further improvement?

EXHIBIT XVII

EMPLOYEE DEVELOPMENT INTERVIEW

(Page 2)

4. What plans do you have for making needed improvement?

5. List specific things you have done within the past twelve months which you feel have contributed to your overall job improvement.

6. How might your supervisor help you improve on the job?

SUPERVISOR COMPLETES THIS SECTION

7. In what skills do you feel the employee needs improvement?

8. What suggestions do you have for making needed improvement?

9. In what areas is the employee's job performance satisfactory?

10. In what areas does the employee need to improve?

day when they stopped for lunch the waitress took the parent's orders first and then asked the boy what he wanted. The mother quickly replied: "Bring him a child's order of roast beef, mashed potatoes, fruit, and a glass of milk."

The waitress, seemingly, failed to hear as she turned to the boy and asked, "Now, what will you have?" The boy promptly replied, "I'd like a hamburger and a chocolate milk shake." As the waitress turned to go she said, "Okay, sonny, that's what it will be."

The mother looked surprised and before she could recover to say anything, the waitress was on her way. As the little boy watched her go into the kitchen, he said, "Gee, Mom, she's wonderful. She thinks I'm a real person."

Some Reasons Supervisors Resist an Appraisal Plan

In spite of the advantages of using employee appraisals, many supervisors prefer not to do so. What are the reasons for this? Here are some that are frequently given.

- "My door is always open." Some supervisors feel that regular employee development appraisal discussions are unnecessary because they talk to their workers every day. They say that they give credit for good work, take corrective measures when necessary, and keep their "door open" at all times. This is good and as it should be. Day-to-day contacts, instructions, and coaching *do* build good relationships. They play a vital part in an employee's acceptance of his supervisor as one for whom he has high respect and to whom he looks for guidance and leadership.

However, even in an acceptable day-to-day coaching situation, workers generally do not know what the supervisor expects of them or what he thinks of their work performance. Also, a worker may have problems that he feels cannot be discussed in casual conversation. He wants to talk with his supervisor but never seems to find a favorable time or the courage to approach him.

Regardless of the kind of discussion, it is sometimes difficult for a worker to be completely candid about his feelings with a supervisor who can influence his salary, his job, and his chances for promotion.

The total picture of supervisor-worker relationships is more than an open-door policy.

• "I don't have the time." Employee development talks *do* take time. Also the pastor, minister of education, or other staff supervisor *do* have important professional duties to perform in addition to their supervisory responsibilities. The heavy professional demands made upon them by church members and others drain their mental and physical energies. Also the "hour glass runs out" too soon and precludes giving adequate consideration for supervisory responsibilities. The situation may be described by imagining the supervisor standing at dead center on a teeter-totter. The plank is balanced, but the moment the supervisor moves toward one side the other side loses weight. This possible imbalance raises the question: how can one perform adequately and efficiently the professional duties of his job and at the same time properly help the staff personnel perform their jobs more efficiently. Some supervisors are so generous with their time that they counsel church members and others to the neglect of their own staff co-workers.

Although employee development talks may not provide all the answers, they do provide one good answer to the staff supervisor's dilemma. Regularly scheduled talks *save* time in the long run.

• "I don't need any more problems." Some supervisors dread workers' questions. They feel that appraisal talks will open up problem situations that are better left alone—like Pandora's box. Theirs is an attitude of letting "sleeping dogs lie." However, evidence to the contrary is strong. Bad feelings tend to become less strong and hurtful to the overall work situation when they are brought out into the open and discussed frankly. Many terminated workers would be serving on the same staffs today had someone taken the time to discuss with them their work problems and related questions.

• "Everything is running smoothly." This may or may not be

true. It may be a hopeful dream. When no immediate urgency exists, supervisors are sometimes lulled into a soft bed of apathy. Then when personnel problems flare, they arise quickly to put out the fire. How much better if supervisors can avoid letting a crisis develop in the work situation.

• "Employee development talks are too difficult for me." This resistance is quite natural. Few people ever become competent enough in appraisal interviews that they can say, "I have arrived." But the fact that he is not completely at ease should not deter the supervisor from fulfilling his responsibilities in this area of his work.

Actually, workers usually respond gladly and willingly to a supervisor's efforts. The face-to-face interview helps the worker to see his progress and position in the overall work of the staff and it also sets the stage for an individualized program of self-development.

Suggestions for Setting Up an Employee Development Plan

A plan for growth gives direction and enhancement for a worker's self-development. A good employee development plan can mean the difference between a mediocre and a "top notch" staff. The pastor and personnel committee work together to prepare a suitable plan. The following suggestions may be helpful in setting it up:

• Keep the plan simple. A plan involves system. How much system is desirable is of prime importance. Provide only enough structure in the system to facilitate the plan and at the same time avoid burdening supervisors with unnecessary paperwork. A one-page (both sides) guide sheet that includes a section for evaluation is a good beginning. Later, as experience dictates, modification of the guide sheet may be desirable and appropriate. See Exhibit XVII for a suggested guide sheet.

• Provide for periodic interviews. Perhaps one or two interviews a year with each worker is ample.

• Establish a date schedule. Set up interview schedules which are several months removed from each worker's pay grade anniversary date. A less inhibited discussion results when the talks are not related to the time of salary increase consideration.

• Keep the plan job-related. The best plan is one that deals directly with the statements of a worker's job description. The employee and the supervisor mutually identify job skills such as typing, filing, editing, posting, receptionist's work, in office and clerical workers' job descriptions. Job skills for professional staff workers may be counseling, planning, organizing, interviewing, visiting prospects, leading conferences, executing planned activities, evaluating results, public speaking, preparing sermons, job instructing. Job skills for manual workers are similarly identified.

If an employee is appraised on ability to perform his job skills, he is more likely to accept suggestions in the give-and-take interview than if he is appraised on personal characteristics. Usually, a discussion of personal traits alone invites argument and misunderstanding, causes a breach in personal relations, or ends in an impasse. The worker is usually placed in a defensive role. Out of such interviews come little, if any, satisfactory feelings of accomplishment by either the worker or the supervisor. This does not mean that a supervisor should not deal with a personality trait which seriously affects a worker's performance or interpersonal relationships. This kind of problem should be dealt with in a straightforward but helpful manner.

• Make the plan staffwide in application. The pastor and the personnel committee must be sure that every supervisor understands the aims and purposes of the plan. It will not work if it is imposed on supervisors. Once accepted, every level of supervision should follow the employee development plan agreed upon. Any omission or deviation tends to diminish its effectiveness.

• Set up procedure. Request each supervisor to be responsible for implementing the plan with his workers. This requires setting up dates with every employee under his supervision. The pastor, as staff leader, may wish to devote a part or all of one staff meeting each year to a discussion of the plan with particular emphasis on results obtained. Annual evaluations usually reveal areas for improvement.

The Employee Development Interview

Planning for an interview.—Regardless of how comfortable the supervisor feels in his day-to-day coaching relationships, he may yet feel inadequate when the time comes for face-to-face work appraisal interviews with his workers. This is normal. The workers usually feel a little nervous, too. Good preplanning on the supervisor's part is highly rewarding in overcoming these anxieties and in helping to develop greater confidence in purposeful discussion. These suggestions may be helpful:

- Set a date and time which is mutually acceptable. Confer with the worker and set a date at least a week in advance. Tell the worker the purpose of the meeting. Ask him to complete his section of the appraisal form and be prepared to talk about his work.
- Check the previous appraisal evaluation, if any. Review job improvement needs previously agreed upon.
- Complete the supervisor's portion of the appraisal form. Write in statements of the employee's work accomplishments, things not accomplished, where improvement is needed, and suggestions for improvement.
- Plan what to say. The supervisor should put himself in the worker's place and think what his reactions would be if his supervisor said the same things to him. Be prepared with facts and suggestions on how improvement can be made. Do not talk in generalities.
- Decide what you want to accomplish. This may include such areas as identifying job skills, clarifying duties, agreeing on priority jobs, discussing areas of needed improvement, suggesting ways for improvement.

Conducting an interview.—The place to conduct the interview is important. If held in the supervisor's office, his desk should be uncluttered. Arrange the chairs so that the conversation can take place across the shortest desk space. This will move the supervisor from behind his desk to the side. This gesture alone adds greatly to establishing an informal atmosphere for the discussion.

Allow ample time for the interview. Ask the receptionist or someone to take any calls.

Greet the worker cordially and make him physically comfortable. Do not apologize for the interview. Get to the discussion without too much delay. Review the purpose of the meeting and assure him you want to talk things over in order to get his job views, ideas, and questions.

The success of the interview rests largely with the supervisor's ability to put himself in the worker's place, to see and to understand things from his point of view. Again, to quote Lawrence A. Appley: "Each employee wants a clear knowledge of what he is expected to do, how well he is expected to do it, how well he is doing it, how he might do it better, and how he might qualify for greater responsibilities."

The supervisor may wish to begin the interview in an area which is very familiar to the employee: his job duties. Ask questions such as: What do you consider some of the most important duties of your job? In which of these duties do you feel you are doing your best work? To which of the skills in your job description do you feel the need of giving more attention and effort? How can I help you do a better job? Questions such as these help to establish rapport between supervisor and employee.

Of course, the above questions are not meant to indicate a one-way conversation; the interview should be a dialogue. In the final analysis, the worker wants to know the supervisor's appraisal of his work. He wants the supervisor to contribute, but he also wants him to listen.

If the supervisor begins the interview by complimenting the employee's work and telling him what a great guy he is and how indispensible he is (even though with truth) the worker becomes suspicious and wonders when the supervisor is going to "lower the boom" with the critical word "but."

In evaluating his work, eliminate reference to an isolated incident in which the worker was involved. No one particularly enjoys being reminded of a mistake, or a blunder, or some act of omission which occurred months ago and was never repeated.

Some do's and don't's during an interview.—Perhaps the following words of caution will be helpful:

- Do let the worker talk; listen while he does so. This helps him understand himself and makes him more receptive to suggestions.
- Do talk about him, not yourself. After all, it is his work appraisal under discussion.
- Do talk about specific things, not generalities. Be sure not to become involved in arguing about the meaning of words. This may cause talking in circles or provoke conflict when no conflict actually exists.
- Do observe what he does not say. Sometimes feelings, attitudes, and motives lie hidden beneath a facade of circumventing statements or questions.
- Don't argue. It leads nowhere. The supervisor may feel that he won his point but the proof lies in the worker's acceptance of it. If the worker becomes defensive, call attention to his reaction without pursuing it further.
- Don't give advice. To say "if I were you" is a conversation stopper. Even if the worker asks for advice, he may not really want it. In such instances, use the nondirective approach by asking, What do you think you should do? If the worker is given advice and accepts it, he may become dependent on the supervisor. If he does not accept it, a barrier may develop.
- Don't permit a situation to develop in which the employee asks all the questions. Control of the discussion, however, does not mean that the supervisor does most of the talking and questioning. The meeting should be one of mutual give-and-take.
- Don't display authority. To say, What you say just isn't so, or, This is what you are going to do, creates disharmony and antagonism. The supervisor who has to display authority in order to show that he is the "boss" has much to learn in developing human relations skills.
- Don't admonish. The comment "I told you so" or "I tried to tell you that wouldn't work" produces nothing but employee resentment.

• Don't display anger. Do not let the worker's feelings cause you to show personal anger. Maintain poise regardless.

• Don't pass the buck. "Passing the buck" is blaming others openly, or in a subtly accusing manner, for the status of things. For example, "I tried to get you a new file case, but you know how hard it is to get anything out of the finance committee" or "I did recommend a salary increase for you two months ago, but the 'powers that be' said they'd review it when they had time." Regardless of how true the "buck passing" statements are, the worker feels that these answers are inadequate. He may even feel that to get anything done he must go directly to the proper committee chairman, or another person, to plead his case.

• Don't permit a worker to criticize other staff employees. He may be looking for a scapegoat or be unwilling to face up to his own inadequacies. Although other workers *may* be involved, it is wise to deal honestly and straightforwardly with one worker at a time. A conflict between two workers requires another kind of meeting, not an employee development appraisal conference.

• Don't close the meeting without mutually reaching work improvement decisions. Perhaps work-flow bottlenecks are causing schedule breakdowns. Perhaps the facility arrangement of the office, or offices, needs study. Or perhaps the person will decide to take a night course in basic grammar.

Every Employee Is Somebody

Why bother to help a staff worker improve and develop on his job? Because every employee is important. He wants job satisfaction, security, credit when credit is due, and assurance that he is making a worthwhile contribution where he works.

But don't expect immediate results from employee development appraisals. The process of helping workers "grow up" on their jobs is slow and unspectacular. It takes time. It may be compared to the growth of the proverbial oak tree. Only over a period of months and years does evidence of growth appear. But in some cases they are dramatic indeed when compared with the worker's initial job efforts.

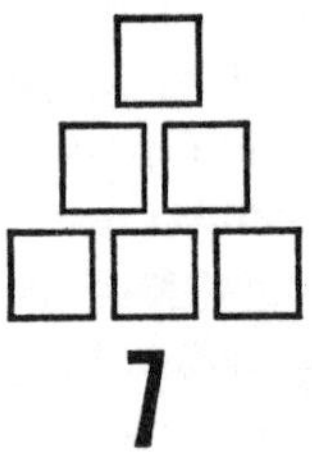

7

Developing Supervisory and Human Relations Skills

In a church with one, two, three, or four workers, the pastor is usually the only staff supervisor. A larger church may have several supervisors in addition to the pastor such as the minister of education, minister of music, business administrator, maintenance foreman. See Exhibit V for sample organization charts.

A person is not a supervisor simply because he has people reporting to him. Perhaps he was assigned the responsibility without having been given the accompanying authority. Or he may never have wanted to be a supervisor in the first place, even though he was made one and with full authority.

If a person inherited a supervisor's job along with professional assignments he may feel no particular responsibility to assume the role of supervisor. To him the professional aspects of his job take precedent over other duties. His motto seems to be: The workers have their jobs and I have mine.

He is like the urbanite who suddenly inherited a farm to which he moved but kept his city job. He did not cultivate the land and later was surprised to see it growing up in weeds and buckbushes. The low morale and work output under such circumstances are painfully obvious.

A hopeful fact is that supervisors are not born supervisors;

they are made. Nor does a person become a full-grown supervisor overnight. He may be assigned a supervisor's title and new responsibilities, but he is the same person. The principal difference is that he is suddenly thrust into an environment involving new and varied human relationships.

The situation may be compared to the young husband at the hospital who is told by the nurse that he is now a father. All of a sudden his job title changes. And all of a sudden, he feels a new responsibility. To be the kind of a father he wants to be will now require a lifetime of guidance, patience, and understanding.

A supervisor makes a most serious error if he assumes a noncommittal, detached attitude toward full acceptance of his supervisory responsibilities. Later, and maybe too late, he discovers that he is reaping a crop of discontent, discord, indifference, and general low morale from among the workers.

For a man to see and accept himself in the role of supervisor is important, if he expects to fill it. In order to do something, it is first necessary to have a concept of it.

This does not mean that the supervisor should spend most of his time directing others, leaving little or no time for the professional aspect of his job. A good supervisor who plans and organizes well, who coordinates various activities, and who delegates responsibilities makes the overall job much easier on himself and on everyone else. Therein lies the secret of good supervision. Consequently, he usually has more time for his professional duties.

Conversely, the church staff supervisor who finds more and more of his time consumed by supervisory details, and less and less time for his professional assignments needs to consider anew how he goes about performing the total requirements of his job. The job may be poorly described, but usually the supervisor is the problem.

Someone has said that people can be placed into three groups: the few who make things happen; the many who watch things happen; and the great majority who have no idea what's happening.

The effective supervisor makes things happen. He is delegated authority to direct the work of others and is responsible for their production. He manages things, activities, and situations, but he gets the job done through people.

The staff supervisor plans, organizes, and coordinates the work of one or more persons, gives instruction and direction, analyzes, interprets, and evaluates results, guides, counsels, and inspires workers to attain their highest potential. He is their leader.

Another important point for a supervisor to realize is that he does not automatically have the respect and loyalty of those whom he supervises simply because he is the supervisor. Workers may respect the office a person holds without respecting the person.

Clarence Francis, former president and chairman of the Board of General Foods, said of supervision: "You can buy a man's time; you can buy a man's physical presence at a given place; you can even buy a measured number of skilled muscular motions per day, but you cannot buy enthusiasm; you cannot buy loyalty; you cannot buy the devotion of hearts, minds, and souls. You have to earn these things."

Some suggestions may help a supervisor "to earn these things."

A Good Supervisor Develops Supervisory Skills

A supervisor is successful in his job to the degree that he develops skills in the following areas:

• Planning. Planning is the determining of a course of action to achieve desired results. Planning is a blueprint for action, and it goes on continually.

Some supervisors are known as planners but not as doers. Their plans never get off the drawing board. To plan for the sake of planning is not enough. Talking about what needs to be done is of first importance, but it is only half of planning. *Doing* is the other half.

As a planner, the supervisor must show imagination, foresight, and sound judgment in forecasting needs and in setting goals. He must work out the essential strategies and necessary actions to attain the goals. He needs to discuss plans with others who are involved and follow through with them. He must evaluate results to discover better ways for subsequent planning.

Some phases of planning may require individual research and design; other phases may best be done as a team effort. Regardless of the method followed, the supervisor, at some step in the planning process, should share the plans with the workers who are to help implement them and ask for their suggestions and comments.

For example, a work-flow problem exists. The supervisor privately studies the problem and decides on a rearrangement of the office facilities. He requests the janitors to change the location of several desks and file cases over the weekend. He may be rather proud of himself as he eagerly awaits the workers' happy comments on Monday morning. Instead, their reactions are chilling indeed. They are most unhappy. There is no comment on the improved work flow, but they gripe and complain because they were "left in the dark" in the planning stage. How much better for all concerned if the supervisor had asked for their suggestions! After all, no one knows better the intricate work-flow problems than do the workers. Chances are that the workers could have made suggestions for rearranging the facilities that would have been an improvement upon the supervisor's effort. Better yet, they not only would probably have approved and accepted the change, but also would have cooperated in making the revised setup work.

A good supervisor gives workers an opportunity to use their judgment, ingenuity, and initiative whenever possible. Suggestions from employees who work with records, files, and machines, or who maintain the buildings often prove to be time and money savers.

It is shocking to realize how much brain power in the workers goes untapped. When a supervisor reserves all the brain work for himself, he may build up his own importance, but he lessens that of his workers. They want to be a part of the team. Teamwork involves planning. Planning involves participation. How can workers give their best when their best is not challenged?

• Organizing. A supervisor is responsible for developing an organization capable of accomplishing desired goals. He must know the overall work functions assigned to him for supervision. He then divides into job units work which can be efficiently performed by the workers whom he supervises. He is responsible for setting up necessary work flow procedures. A good organization enables people to work together as a team.

A capable supervisor must be an efficient organizer. Organization helps him to get on top of his job and stay there. He sets a good example. His office, desk, files, and dictation are well organized. He organizes the professional as well as the supervisory aspects of his job. This does not mean he "worships" efficiency. Rather, he recognizes that greater efficiency in getting the job done emerges from setting up proper and adequate schedules, work flow, work procedures, and so forth. To him organization is a tool, a means to an end.

• Coordinating. The supervisor is a coordinator. He adjusts, adapts, and synchronizes the efforts of his group to meet work schedules, deadlines, and goals. Coordination takes place when the supervisor brings workers, materials, and equipment together to accomplish desired work goals. Discoordination causes one to be like the proverbial man who got on his horse and rode off in all directions.

A supervisor can be rated as a coordinator. Does he make some real effort to coordinate the work? Does he generally coordinate well with only occasional lapses? Does he demonstrate skill in work coordination?

• Motivating. To motivate is to lead and inspire workers to their highest possible work attainment.

Some supervisors believe that money and things are the worker's highest motivators. To say that an employee is not influenced by the check in his pay envelope is foolish. However, money alone does not motivate an employee to do his best. In fact, the supervisor who measures a worker's loyalty, cooperation, and dedication solely in terms of salary can never pay enough money.

Through personnel research industry has found that employees place several "wants" ahead of wages. Some of these are job security, job satisfaction, recognition, and good supervision.

For most individuals, the greatest satisfaction and strongest motivation are derived from achievement, responsibility, growth, earned recognition, and work itself. When an employee is motivated by these, he is happily identified with his job.

Supervision, then, plays a significant role in the proper work motivation of an employee. One big job of a supervisor is to know why people act as they do. Knowing a worker's motives and goals helps him to understand the *why* of the worker's behavior.

People vary greatly in their likes, dislikes, personality makeup, life's goals, and so forth. Since people are very complex, the wise supervisor deals with them as individuals. Usually, when workers cooperate and perform as a superb team, the underlying explanation lies in the supervisor's skill and ability to treat them as important individuals. A good supervisor does not push people down; he lifts them up.

An effective supervisor provides each new worker with job information and plans carefully his overall job orientation. For all workers, the supervisor provides incentives for maintaining high performance, encourages the exercise of independent judgment, fosters and invites ideas for better ways to perform the work, gives recognition for work well done, and creates a climate of permissiveness in which the worker knows he is expected to learn from his own mistakes. The supervisor is the key person in the motivation process.

• Controlling. Control means to guide an activity or a project in the direction it is intended to go.

For example, a supervisor controls when he examines, investigates, and evalutes the progress of a project against predetermined time schedules. He checks to see if everything is in order. If not, there may still be time to take whatever action is necessary to correct the unsatisfactory progress of the work plan.

Any supervisor, who waits until deadline dates before he examines the progress of a project, may find that he is in a most embarrassing position. He may censure the workers assigned to the project as a way of releasing his personal feelings. Or, if time yet remains, he may counsel with them about the stage of the project and secure their suggestions and help in doing whatever is necessary to complete the project on schedule. A supervisor demonstrates maturity when he reacts quickly to a crisis and takes positive remedial action. His maturity may be questioned, however, if he lives from one crisis to another. Some supervisors soon learn that periodical checking on the progress of various projects and activities is far better than pampering ulcers.

Sometimes the supervisor may assign responsibility for checking the progress of an activity to another staff worker. If this person is so instructed, he makes the necessary reports, verbal or written, and takes corrective actions when unsatisfactory conditions occur.

One obvious control is the financial budget. The supervisor should study the monthly or quarterly financial reports carefully to ascertain his actual expenditures against those budgeted. The financial statement also reveals unexpended budgeted funds which serve as a guide as well as a control for future activities and their costs.

The five skills named above comprise the main part of a supervisor's work. From them several of his job description statements emerge. He plans, organizes, and coordinates projects, activities, work procedures and schedules. He inspirits the workers. He checks (controls) the progress of projects.

The word "plan" in a job description statement tells the supervisor that he *is* to plan, but it does not tell him *how* to plan. His success in carrying out the intent of the duty depends upon the degree of skill he demonstrates in the "planning process." In this context, "plan" is not a trite action verb prefixed to a duty statement, but it becomes the central force around which the duty takes on significant meaning and purpose.

The answer to the question How proficient are you in planning, or in organizing, or in motivating? obviously lies in the effective results produced through the use of these skills.

The supervisor is the most important person in the work life of those whom he supervises. Supervision is not a lazy man's job.

A Good Supervisor Is a Leader

Practically every day brings something new to which human beings must adjust. They turn to a leader for guidance and help. Under today's pressures, old concepts of leadership are challenged. A leader is no longer a man of great physical strength who imposes his will by sheer force. Rather, workers turn to the man who leads by working with and through them.

To be selected as a supervisor indicates that someone gave credence to one's leadership ability or potential. Leadership may be defined as the art of influencing others to cooperate toward some mutually desirable goal. A leader stimulates the pattern of behavior in a group. There are two divergent approaches to leadership:

The leader-centered approach. The leader decides, on the basis of his presumed superior knowledge and experience, what is best for the group. He uses methods designed to influence members to accept his decisions.

The group-centered approach. This approach involves enhancing the group rather than its leader. In this approach the leader uses the available resources of the members to reach the best group decisions possible.

At least four types of leaders emerge from these two leadership approaches:

- Autocratic. This leader makes the decisions, takes few people into his confidence, and generally keeps authority and responsibility vested in himself. He gives orders and expects them to be obeyed without question. He is the boss! Insecure leaders tend to be autocratic.
- Paternalistic. This leader is similar to the one described above except that he assumes a "father knows best" attitude and sugarcoats all his directives. He does favors for the group and

expects them to be grateful to him. He expects them to carry out his wishes and is offended if they do not—". . . and after all I've done for them."

• Laissez-faire. This leader is one who does not take seriously his leadership responsibility. He is inclined to let the group coast along as it will without too much interference or direction. Whatever a worker or the group of workers want to do is OK with him if that is what they want.

• Democratic. The democratic leader is more difficult to describe. He sees himself as a leader-member of the group. He desires to enhance the group rather than to promote himself. He uses the participative process to stimulate the members of the group to do their best thinking in providing possible problem solutions or better ways in which to perform the work. He respects each person as an individual in his own right.

If one does not know which kind of leader he is, his workers do.

The importance of knowing the various types of leadership is to be able to understand and adjust to a new work environment in which one is placed. Especially is this true when moving to a new church field.

For example, suppose that the workers in the new field are accustomed to strong directive leadership. Suppose further that the new leader is democratic. The question arises: How can he graduate his approach and help the workers to change from a directive to a permissive leadership? Chances are that if he started by using the democratic process, the workers in the group would not know how to "read" him, would become frustrated, and would want their "old" leader back.

Conversely, a group accustomed to working with a strongly permissive leadership will frequently show signs of rebellion when a new leader attempts autocratic domination.

However, even where democracy prevails in a situation, the leader, on occasion, may need to use the authoritarian approach. Leadership styles will vary, depending on the circumstances.

Two main factors in recognizing potentially effective leaders

are adventuresomeness and self-concept control. The adventuresome person likes to meet people, is active, genial, friendly, and responsive. He does not feel threatened by others nor does he feel inferior to them. The second factor, self-concept control, means that he has good feelings about himself. He has self-respect and willpower. He is highly organized in his way of life. Popular leadership is denoted by strong inner controls over emotional reactions and by generally considerate behavior.

The ultimate test of leadership is the effective accomplishment of a job. However, to judge a person by group effectiveness alone may be unfair. He may be limited by the abilities of the workers under his supervision. Also, a group of highly skilled employees may perform acceptably well even though they are ineffectively led.

Every person has some personal leadership—influence with a fellow worker, a neighbor, a golfing or bowling partner, or members of his own family. Personal influence is desirable, of course, but it does not provide the "thrust" that sustained periods of leadership demand.

Personal leadership may be compared to a parked jet airliner. The passenger capacity and speed statistics are impressive. However, as long as the airplane is parked on the apron, the full potential and purpose of the plane remain dormant. Not until the thrust of the engines moves the plane forward toward planned objectives do the statistics come alive.

Some people live a lifetime on the apron of leadership. They have leadership potential but somehow never learn that they could move out on the runway.

A leader should know the areas in which he is weak, average, or strong. He should know the stimuli which usually cause him satisfaction or irritation. He should know his mannerisms, biases, prejudices, and attitudes which are likely to please or irritate others. He should know his own needs, desires, and life's goals. He should know how changes in his physical states and emotional levels affect his attitudes and should allow for them in dealing rationally with others.

A good leader avoids unnecessary collisions with the views of others. He is a good listener and makes every effort to understand and appreciate the opinions of everyone involved in a situation.

There is nothing magical about leadership. To be a leader requires a constant program of self-discipline, self-analysis, and self-improvement. To lead requires energy and courage and, above all, faith in people. It is almost axiomatic that leaders beget leaders. How fortunate indeed when a group of people have a good leader.

A Good Leader Learns from His Mistakes

The sign on the desk read: You may go home now—you've already made enough mistakes for one day.

What an easy way to solve problems! If going home would erase the mistakes, going home is sound advice. However, the mistakes of the day, week, or month have a way of shadowing us wherever we go.

A mistake is the result of misjudgment. Misjudgments are risks taken in decision-making, and church supervisors make decisions every day. Some are major decisions; others are minor. Some supervisors base their decisions on hunches or personal prejudices which cloud rational, logical thinking.

Other supervisors make decisions off the cuff. They do not know exactly why they make them, and not until later, when the decision backfires or when a study of facts reveals a better decision, is the earlier judgment labeled a mistake. Sometimes a person must make a serious blunder before he will take self-inventory. For the moment at least, he knows he does not want to make that same mistake again.

No one deliberately wants to make mistakes, but everyone makes them. Some people make more than others. In fact, there are those who seem to be mistake-prone as some are accident-prone. The harder they try not to make mistakes, the more they seem to make.

However, most people are sympathetic with the misjudgments that staff supervisors make, and try to be understanding. This is

fortunate. There comes a time, though, when sympathy and understanding are somewhat strained.

How do employees of a church staff react to a supervisor who is guilty of recurring mistakes? Here are some possible evaluations:

He is incapable of learning from his mistakes.

He uses poor judgment.

He is indecisive.

Fortunately, most supervisors have discovered that they can learn from their own mistakes as well as from the mistakes of others. Here are some suggestions to aid in this learning process:

• Admit the mistake. Acknowledging a mistake is the first step toward correction, improvement, and development. Mistakes can be good teachers. Workers respect the supervisor who is courageous enough to admit it when he is wrong.

• Analyze the mistake. Think a while about a recent blunder that was made. Did pressure force a decision? Some decisions require time for thinking, weighing facts, and anticipating possible consequences. Was pressure the reason for misjudgment? Do not be pressured into hasty decisions merely out of a desire to appear decisive to a fellow worker or church member. Ask for additional information if necessary, or say specifically that more time is needed to think things through. A supervisor must make many minor decisions daily as problems arise.

Remember that one's mental or physical condition on the day of the decision could be a possible clue.

Reflect upon the circumstances that immediately preceded the instance of judgment. Were they important? Would the same mistake probably be made under similar circumstances? The successful supervisor tries to undo mistakes, but not before carefully analyzing them.

• Consider the nature of the error. How serious is the mistake? Will it affect others? If so, to what extent? Should you disregard the error? And if you do, will the mistake take root and grow?

Sometimes the overly conscientious person broods over and

bemoans all his mistakes. Such an attitude affects his overall work. He subconsciously becomes indecisive for fear of making other mistakes. He creates a false leadership.

Conversely, the effective supervisor is concerned. He studies carefully the nature of each error and boldly faces the consequences. Once a decision is reached, he acts.

• If necessary, discuss the mistake with your own supervisor. This involves judgment. When admission of error to supervisor or pastor becomes necessary, try to think in terms of him and the church, rather than yourself. He wants to know the nature of the mistake, its results, and what is proposed as an alternate. Out of this experience of sharing feelings usually come understanding and support.

To learn from mistakes may mean a revision of past decisions when similar problems or situations arose. Revising decisions when one is shown to be wrong takes courage. Usually, people tend to forget past errors when one shows by current decisions that he has learned by his mistakes.

A Good Supervisor Brings Out the Best in People

How does a person feel when, after one or more years on the job, his supervisor still calls him by the wrong name?

What would be an employee's work attitude if, time after time, good work on assignments had been done and the supervisor never had said, "That was a good job"?

Or, how long could a person tolerate a situation where every voiced desire of the supervisor was an order, or a demand, instead of a request?

Or, how would one feel after returning from an extended illness if the supervisor hardly recognized his presence?

Little things! And perhaps they are. But somehow it's the little things done by a supervisor on a day-to-day basis that people remember and which contribute greatly to bringing out their best. For some supervisors, this is an enigma.

There is a big difference in being thoughtful of others—showing common courtesies—and pampering them.

Supervisors often show by small acts of commission or omission that they are not really interested in each person as an individual. Workers become keenly aware and resentful of their seeming robot existence. Some supervisors are tight-lipped with their words of praise. When deserved praise is not expressed, the worker's motivations to perform efficiently are appreciably dulled.

Yet other supervisors create an atmosphere of fear as a motivation for getting the work done. Whether or not the supervisor does so intentionally makes little difference to the worker who daily feels fear pressures. Generally, people do not perform at their best under an umbrella of fear.

The attitude of the supervisor is extremely important—attitude in terms of people as they are related to their work. A good supervisor knows he can develop a better team when he blends an employee- and production-centered style of leadership. However, the supervisor who attempts to substitute a superficial interest in the worker in order to get production is not fooling anyone but himself. The workers detect insincerity and resent manipulation.

How can supervisors, who come in all shapes and sizes, who bring to their jobs certain specific knowledge and skills, and who have varying attitudes, emotions, likes, and dislikes, bring out the best in people? Several suggestions are:

• Show a genuine interest in workers. To know their names is not enough; know their problems also. Understand workers and their reactions. Provide opportunity for employee development and self-improvement. Show patience, tolerance, and understanding. Treat workers as human beings. Show respect for their feelings. A friendly manner and kindly guidance win cooperation. When a supervisor shows a genuine interest in people, they usually respond through improved work attitude and production.

• Communicate clearly. Nothing is quite so frustrating to a worker as garbled instruction. Result: waste of time and loss of job motivation. On the other hand, clear, easily understood instructions create mutual confidence between the worker and the supervisor. Job confidence is a requisite to top performance.

• Observe rules of courtesy. A "please" makes the assignment seem less like an order or a demand. The words "thank you" require no extra effort but pave the way for heartier cooperation. Courtesy promotes mutual respect, goodwill, and helps greatly to bring out the best in people.

• Criticize in the right way. No one likes to be criticized openly where others can hear. A good supervisor does not cause a worker to lose face or self-respect. He criticizes in private. He criticizes in a constructive manner. He always leaves the person thinking well of himself. If the supervisor has no ready answer or solution, he should probably remain silent until he does.

• Give credit when credit is due. When a supervisor gives credit to another, he gains credit himself. A supervisor who does not praise those with whom he works soon finds himself working twice as hard and getting less cooperation. A worker sometimes expresses appreciation for a fellow employee. Such consideration is commendable. However, nothing satisfies quite as much as when the supervisor says, "Thank you for the good job you did."

• Fulfil promises. A good supervisor is careful about the promises he makes. However, once he makes a promise, he must keep it in order to be known as a man of his word.

• Resolve complaints promptly and fairly. A problem or complaint of a worker should be very real and important to the supervisor. The worker wants an explanation, an answer, or action. He is quite sensitive to the degree of the supervisor's interest and willingness to set up an appointment to discuss the matter. A good supervisor arranges a time for private talk as soon as possible. He listens to the worker. He resolves the complaint or problem in a way that is fair to *all* concerned. The worker with the complaint may or may not agree with the solution. However, the more important questions are: Does this worker feel that he received a fair hearing? Does he feel that another worker with the same complaint would have received the same answer.

• Treat workers impartially. Perhaps no one act of the supervisor breaks down morale more quickly than showing favoritism. To give one worker a day off now and then but to refuse others the same privilege invites problems by the dozen. Acts of favoritism, however subtle, create conflict, antagonism, and cause a general breakdown of morale. The good supervisor brings out the best in people by impartial and considerate treatment.

• Treat workers fairly. Supervisors are sometimes confused in their dealings with other humans. In the turmoil created by unexpected situations, their confusion is somewhat like that of the man who stepped off the curb while the traffic light was changing. In that brief moment a motorist who speeded up to get across the intersection splashed him with mud and water. As the man jumped back on the curb, he exclaimed excitedly to two bystanders, "Did you two fools see what that gentleman just did to me?"

He was confused, but no more mixed up than are some supervisors in everyday situations which make sudden demands to deal fairly with people.

A person's estimate or measure of his own sense of fairness may or may not be in agreement with those whom he supervises. Workers are sensitive to observable or knowledgeable inequities in so-called fair treatment.

Most supervisors would rate high on some of the *major* aspects of fair treatment of others. Some examples are: not telling a deliberate falsehood about a fellow worker; not intentionally assigning the hardest job to a certain employee to hasten his termination; or not knowingly claiming credit for something a worker under his supervision accomplished.

But how would these same supervisors rate when *little* things that count for so much are involved? Such as:

Criticizing a worker for a mistake when inquiry reveals that he had not been adequately instructed

Making a careless remark about a worker before another and thus creating adverse opinion

Deciding not to give an employee a salary increase because of one recent unfavorable incident

Calling together all the workers to reprimand them collectively when only one is at fault, or,

Giving one employee his choice of vacation time and then asking the others to choose their times so as not to be in conflict.

The achievement of fairness in both big and little things requires constant striving. Intent is involved, of course, but intent in itself is not enough. There is no halfway in fairness.

Another important area affecting human relations involves the fair treatment of all employees in the administration of the church's employee benefit plan.

Although an employee may be unhappy to find that the benefits he receives are less than those received by workers in other churches, his real discontent is caused by the knowledge that he is not treated the same as other workers in his own group. Confidence of fair treatment is of prime concern to the employee.

When is a worker treated unfairly in the administration of employee benefits? Generally speaking, unfairness results when no rhyme or reason exists to explain why one or more workers are excluded from some staff benefits, or why there are wide variances in benefits to be shared by all. A worker who does not understand the employee benefit plan may not raise his voice to question a seeming inequity. However, quiet acceptance does not necessarily imply happy acceptance.

No one likes to be treated unfairly. The supervisor who knowingly or unknowingly engages in unfair treatment practices is usually demanding in seeking justice for himself. One of the major "wants" of every employee is to work in a place where he is treated fairly. Such treatment helps to bring out the best in people.

Rate yourself on the chart below.

Exhibit XVIII

How Do I Rate as a Supervisor?

This questionnaire will help the supervisor make a candid and useful evaluation of essential characteristics of good supervisory leadership. Make an honest self-appraisal when rating each item (weak, 1; average, 2; strong, 3; superior, 4). When all items are rated, total your score. (Total perfect score is 100.)

	Score
1. Do I understand the work of those I supervise?	( )
2. Do I use the abilities of those I supervise?	( )
3. Am I always fair in my dealings with employees?	( )
4. Do I have a "listening ear" for their problems?	( )
5. Do I keep the promises I make?	( )
6. Do I give credit when credit is due?	( )
7. Do I seek advice from workers in planning that involves them?	( )
8. Do I let each worker know where he stands in his work?	( )
9. Do I inform workers in advance of changes that affect them?	( )
10. Do I gain the worker's confidence (earn loyalty and trust?)	( )
11. Do I listen to the ideas of my workers?	( )
12. Do I explain the "why" of things that are to be done?	( )
13. Do I admit the mistakes I make?	( )
14. Do I criticize constructively?	( )
15. Do I set a good work example before my workers?	( )
16. Am I consistent in my actions before my workers?	( )
17. Do I show confidence in my workers?	( )
18. Do I try to resolve complaints?	( )
19. Do I "back up" my workers?	( )
20. Do I keep my temper when workers make mistakes?	( )
21. Do I accept criticism in a good spirit?	( )
22. Do I show concern for others?	( )
23. Do I properly instruct each worker?	( )
24. Do I constantly pursue a plan of self-improvement?	( )
25. Do I encourage self-improvement of my workers?	( )
Total Score	( )

Human relations is more than smiling at people. Working with people is an art. Basic attitudes which comprise a philosophy of life are more significant than the techniques used. However, techniques used appropriately and sincerely are highly endorsed and encouraged.

Human relations is more than giving service to church members. Service without heart, understanding, and personal interest is like tinkling silver and sounding brass.

Human relations is not achieved by status: a walnut desk, carpet, and matched appointments. Human relationships are not achieved with things; but rather, they exist between people. An attractive and orderly office is helpful in creating a climate for giving efficient and friendly service, of course. But when a person depends upon things to give him status, he tends to grow inward and become dwarfed.

Few people attain high levels in human relations skills. Yet the rules are so simple that they can be used easily by anyone who sincerely desires to improve. However, it is one thing to know the rules and quite another to apply them. The supervisor's success in human relations skills waits upon putting desire into action.

"Finally, you must all live in harmony, be sympathetic, loving as brothers, tender-hearted, humble, never returning evil for evil or abuse for abuse, but blessing instead" (1 Peter 3: 8–9, Williams).

A Good Supervisor Desires to Be a Better Supervisor

"Well, did you learn anything today?" the teen-ager asked as her six-year-old brother sauntered in from his first day at school.

"No, not much," he replied, as he continued his way to the refrigerator. "Guess I'll have to go back tomorrow."

What a profound answer! Not only tomorrow, but many tomorrows—as long as he lives—he will be in some sort of school. The only difference that time makes is the change from education as such, which is ordinarily quite broad in scope, to one or more specific training and improvement objectives related directly to the job.

Persons in almost all fields of professional activity must continue to study beyond their formal education if they are to keep pace with changing concepts, improved methods, and applications. The church paid staff supervisor is no exception.

The man who, upon graduation, says to himself, "I finally made it; now I can rest awhile," is like the person who rows to the middle of a placid lake and then pulls in his oars. Although the impetus of years of formal training may carry a person forward for a time, he soon becomes aware that he must reactivate the oars of study to move forward—even to maintain—his position as a leader.

The statement of a baseball player, Satchel Paige, "Never look back; something may be gaining on you," may be appropriate advice. The forward look is important to the fulfilment of a person's life purposes.

The better trained a person is the more productive he can be. This does not necessarily mean that a well-trained person *will* be more productive, but it does mean that he *can* be more productive. His "drive" factors depend largely upon how much incentive his job furnishes for the achievement of top performance.

Every man's self-development is an individual matter. The best laboratory is the job itself where a man's development is largely the result of his day-to-day work experiences. This does not mean that putting in the hours over a period of time will automatically develop a supervisor into a full-blown leader in his field. When ten years have passed, he may find that all he has had is one year of experience repeated ten times.

How can a supervisor grow and develop on the job? The following suggestions may be helpful:

• Analyze the job duties. What are the responsibilities? Write them down. Some supervisors may say, "I know what I'm supposed to do. Why do I need to write job statements?" There are several reasons:

To make certain that all the duties of the job are receiving proportionate attention and emphasis. Otherwise, he may tend to perform only in those areas which he most enjoys and to avoid those he does not like.

To check the job duties with his own supervisor and to reach full agreement as to the accuracy of the statements. Agreement helps to avoid future uncomfortable moments of interpersonal misundersanding.

Use the following as a basis for a plan of self-development.

• Analyze the skills required by the job description. A supervisor's main job is to plan, organize, coordinate, direct, and control the work under his supervision. He also has responsibilities related to the professional side of his job.

The job description includes statements which identify supervisory-professional responsibilities. A careful study of job statements reveals the skills required for successful performance.

For example, the supervisor's impact of leadership upon the thoughts and actions of others expresses itself through his ability to write to individuals; speak to groups; lead conferences; organize groups; plan programs; set up schedules of activities and work flow; enlist and train workers; visit members and prospects; conduct staff meetings; interview applicants; coordinate activities; plan and control budgets; evaluate results.

A supervisor could rate himself in each of the above actions (and others) by using the following evaluations:

My strongest point
Fairly skilled in this one
I need to work on this one
I really need to work on this one
May be the cause of some of my problems

Perhaps another helpful way toward self-development would be to review the following questions and make whatever personal application is necessary:

Do I present problems or solutions?
Do I finish a job?
Do I know when a job is finished?
Do I meet deadlines?

Do my meetings get results?
Do I lack initiative?
Do I know how to bring out the best in people?
Do I "worship" efficiency?
Do I know how to listen?
Do I have difficulty getting my ideas across?
Do I know how to say what I mean?
Do I think before I speak?
Do I follow through on things I agree to do?
Do I maintain regular work schedules?
Do I know how to plan a talk?
Do I know how to lead a conference?
Do I waste today's energy stewing over yesterday's decisions?
Do I have difficulty in making decisions?
Do I try to do a little bit of everything?
Do I have difficulty delegating responsibility?
Do I find the morning is gone with little or no work done?

• Select two or three of the job skills in the description in which improvement is needed—for example, more effectiveness in leading conferences. How could a program of improvement be planned? What items would be included? What sort of a time schedule could be set up? How could actual skill improvement in leading conferences be evaluated?

The improvement plan might include reading several books on conference leading and attending a seminar or workshop on the subject. After even casual study, improvement in subsequent conference leadership is often revealed. Give close attention to conference room mannerisms, behavior, and habits which negate best results. Sometimes, in spite of all resolves beforehand, and conscious efforts during the conference itself, some hopefully shelved habits reappear during the proceedings. Don't despair. Try again. This is important to self-development.

Everyone needs to increase his effectiveness in one or more job skills. Effectiveness can be acquired first, by a recognition of the need, second, by a desire to improve, and third, by doing something about it. Generally, poor work habits make a supervisor-professional worker ineffective on his job—not a lack of ability.

However, attending conferences, workshops, and so forth indiscriminately for the sake of accumulating hours is not efficient self-development planning. Learning by trial and error alone is usually a waste of time. Rather, a self-development program should be planned, scheduled, and carried out systematically.

Self-development, then, is best learned through a direct application of knowledge and skills to the requirements of the job.

Since a supervisor cannot create more hours in the day, his only choice is to order these hours so as to be more effective in fulfilling the demands of his work.

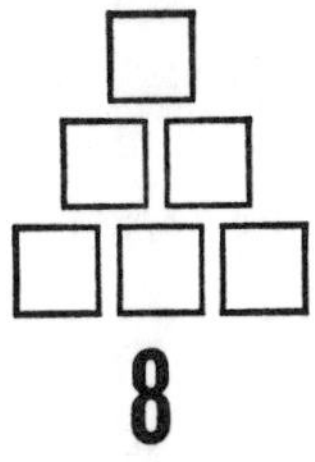

8

Planning and Conducting Effective Staff Meetings

When someone asked a small boy what was the purpose of a cow's hide, he replied, "To hold the cow together." In a very real sense, one outcome of good staff meetings is to hold the staff together. These meetings can form an integral part of the work life of paid employees by binding them together as a unit. Staff meetings can give purpose and direction to the overall work of the staff.

Although fellowship is involved, the purpose of staff meetings is for more than fellowship, or for devotional services—as important as they are, or for checking the weekly calendar of activities, or for reviewing the results of the past Sunday.

Basically, a staff meeting is a medium of communication. It is not an end in itself; it is a means to an end. However, a meeting of the staff should not be used for every communication situation which arises among workers. There are times when a memo serves the purpose or talking individually to those specifically concerned with a work problem may be better.

The optimum value of a staff meeting lies in the change it produces in the participants such as knowledge, attitude, behavior, and work habits.

Someone has said, "Committees keep minutes, but waste

hours." Another has commented, "A camel is a horse put together by a committee." These two observations reveal a simple fact: some meetings are a waste of time, poorly planned, and nonproductive.

Why conduct staff meetings? Are they worth the time and effort? The answer is a positive *yes*. Purposeful staff meetings are extremely important to the support of the overall church program cycle of planning, organizing, executing, and evaluating projects and activities. There are several reasons for conducting staff meetings:

- They help to positionize and identify each staff member as a part of the team. He feels that he belongs. His identity as a team member is important to him. Staff meetings help him get into the act.
- They serve as a mortar to hold the group together. Good rapport is basic to concerted action.
- They spark employee self-development. Out of group interaction often come incentives which motivate workers to pursue further study in their field, or related fields, of work.
- They serve as a means of establishing goals, developing strategies, and determining actions, of solving problems, developing policies and procedures, analyzing data, coordinating activities, and stimulating ideas.

The pastor is responsible for planning and conducting meetings comprising the total paid staff or any segment of it as required to accomplish the meeting's objectives.

Each supervisor, such as the minister of education, church business administrator, minister of music, is responsible for planning and conducting necessary meetings involving the workers he supervises directly.

How Often Should Staff Meetings Be Scheduled?

As often as needed is a good answer to this question, but it may not be the best one. There are some pastors, or other staff supervisors who seldom, if ever, plan staff meetings because they personally feel no need for them. Usually, none of the others on the staff share this feeling. In fact, in some churches where there are no staff meetings, the workers usually say to one another, "If we could just get together once in a while to solve some of our work problems," or "If we just knew what was going on," or "Maybe we could do a better job if all of us were pulling in the same direction."

Two extremes seem to exist: not having any meetings, or scheduling them daily or weekly without preplanning. To the question, When do you hold staff meetings? a survey disclosed these responses:

We do not have staff meetings
No special time
Whenever a staff meeting is needed
Every Monday morning
Once a month

A few churches in the survey indicated a regular daily session. By far the greatest percent indicated that they held regular weekly meetings. Every day in the work week was mentioned, but Monday was the most popular time. According to this survey, comparatively few staff meetings were held in the afternoon. The morning hours between 8:30–11:00 were most frequently named.

How Plan Staff Meetings?

Scheduling is not planning. The real challenge for staff leaders who conduct meetings is to give thoughtful consideration to the following:

• Define the meeting's purpose. Think through these questions: Why have this meeting? What do we hope to accomplish in this meeting? Keep in mind that, since a meeting serves only as a medium of communication, the actual results are usually reached later, not at the meeting itself.

When the reason for the meeting is determined, write it down. If a problem is to be solved, be sure to state it clearly.

• Get facts beforehand. They may be readily available from the files, or they may require research. Do not assume that, without prior notice, a worker in the meeting will have all the facts at his fingertips. Not only is the delay in getting facts a waste of the time of those who wait, but it is also a source of embarrassment to the person who was not able to produce facts "off the cuff." When a meeting continues without vital facts, the conferees may reach an impasse, or debate in circles, or make a decision on the basis of guesswork.

Not every meeting requires the gathering of facts beforehand. Planning, however, can spotlight the need for this or for other areas of advance preparation needed.

• Determine the type of meeting to be conducted. The role which the leader assumes in the meeting depends largely on the objectives to be accomplished. Is the purpose of the meeting to inform ("tell and sell") a decision already made, or to pool considered opinions, ideas, and facts for decision-making, or for collecting information?

Each type (to inform and persuade, or to solve a problem) requires a different leadership role. For example, if the purpose of the meeting is to inform others of a decision already reached by the leader, or by a church committee, one simply tells the workers what was decided. In this instance, the meeting is informational. The leader's role, basically, is one of relaying instructions, explaining decisions or actions already formulated, answering the conferee's questions, and motivating (sell) the participant to acceptance. In this type of meeting, counter arguments or suggestions for possible improvement by the conferees are out of place. The matter is already settled. It is entirely possible that if counter proposals are offered by the conferees, the leader, at the beginning, did not communicate clearly to them the purpose of the meeting.

If the purpose of the meeting is to solve a problem, the leader assumes a different role. He states the problem, gives opportunity for discussion, examines the facts, hears possible solutions, and either selects the best solution and an alternate, or shares this responsibility with the group. See next page for seating arrangement and communication flow in various types of meetings.

SUGGESTED ARRANGEMENT OF TABLES AND CHAIRS

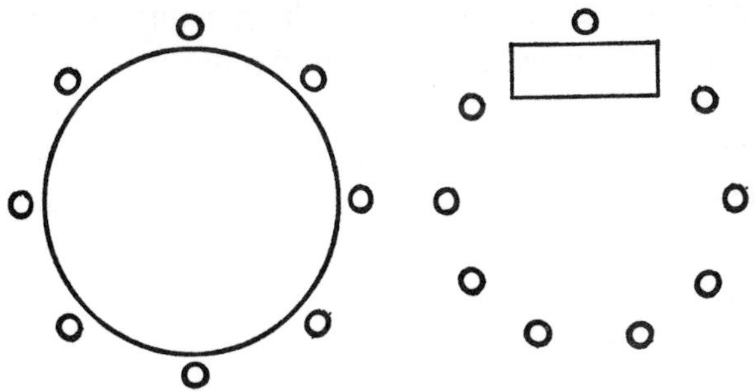

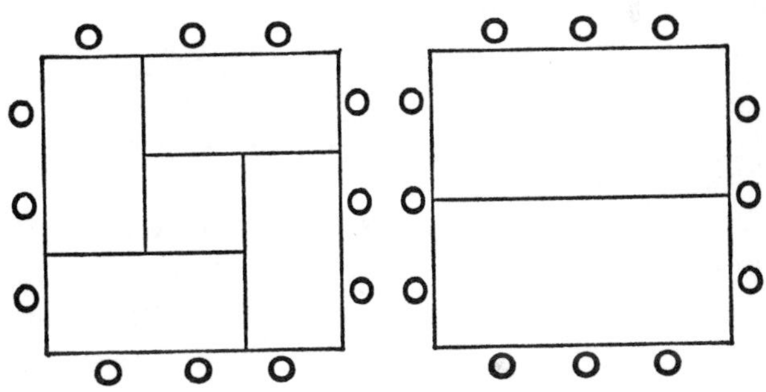

GROUP INTERACTION

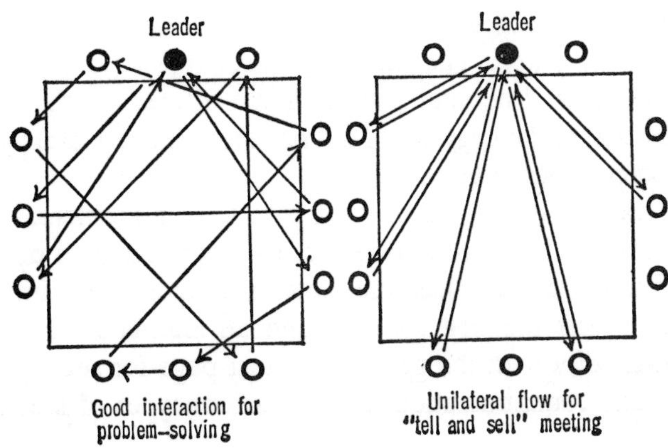

Good interaction for problem-solving

Unilateral flow for "tell and sell" meeting

Who Attends Staff Meetings?

The purpose of the meeting determines who should attend. If it is principally for devotion and fellowship, especially at the beginning of the session, perhaps all paid workers, including the custodians and maids, should be present.

However, if the purpose is for matters such as: to solve a problem, make plans, coordinate projects and activities, establish goals, strategies, and actions, then only those staff members who have definite responsibilities in these areas should attend. They are the ones qualified to have opinions. They are the workers who have the facts, or who are in charge of a project or projects, or who will carry out group decisions, or whose work becomes involved later on.

A poor stewardship of time is to ask clerical workers to sit through an hour's session involving discussions which are of little or no interest to them. If "sitting through the meeting" is required of all staff members, some of the clerical workers will certainly develop an apathetic attitude toward them. They can't wait to get back to their work, especially if it is piled high on their desks.

On the other hand, if an item on the agenda involves developing better interoffice communication procedure, the clerical workers, especially those who answer the telephones, should be present to participate in the discussion. After the matter is settled, the clerical workers can be excused to return to their desks.

On a smaller church staff comprising three, four, or five workers, the pastor may wish all workers to remain for the entire session, largely because of the close relationship and interrelated work involvements.

It is the responsibility of the pastor (or the supervisor for his own group) to arrange the time and place of the meeting. Choose a place with ample space, good lighting, chairs, and chalkboard. Select a room away from the telephone, if possible.

Notify the workers in advance of the meeting date. Tell them the purpose of the meeting if there are problems to discuss.

Another important item in preparing for the meeting is to get together necessary materials such as records, charts, pamphlets, chalk, eraser, pencils, paper.

How Conduct a Staff Meeting?

Although thorough preparation is necessary for an effective meeting, that alone does not insure success. There must be purposeful participation by all members. The mutual give and take (interactions) of the conferees, their awareness, sensitivity, and diagnostic skill—all these largely determine the success of a meeting.

To increase the chances for a successful meeting, add to good preparation these suggestions:

- Start on time. Begin with prayer.
- Define the type of meeting: informational, problem-solving, or other. This step is unnecessary, of course, for staff meetings that are primarily devotional. If the meeting is for problem-solving, state the problem clearly. Give background information that would help the group to understand the problem.
- Open the discussion. To get the discussion started, ask pertinent questions to arouse interest and provoke thinking. The leader does not necessarily need to be an expert on the subject for discussion. Rather, he should be skilled in the use of the democratic process.

Some leaders employ a pseudodemocratic method in leading a problem-solving conference. This means that the leader already has the solution in mind. He merely goes through the motions of a democratic process. By pulling from the conferees an opinion which, in reality, voices his predetermined solution he hopes to make them think that it is theirs. This manipulation is deeply resented by the participants when it is discovered.

When a problem-solving meeting is so identified, the leader must proceed honestly with the group and follow the democratic process toward reaching a decision. If he has ideas to contribute, he should present them for evaluation and discussion, but not in a manner to make others feel that he is structuring the meeting.

Reluctance on the part of the leader to trust the mental capacities of others prompts them to distrust the leader.

• Get everyone into the act. Encourage participation and mutual exchange of experiences, opinions, and ideas. Create an atmosphere in which each one feels free to take part in the discussion.

How does a leader secure group interaction? How does he lead the group to look carefully at all four corners of a problem? How does he lead them to a quality group decision?

These questions have no "pat" answers. A leader must reckon with a wide gamut of individual differences. A person may be a recognized leader in one situation and a lukewarm participant in another. Each conferee relates in varied and peculiar ways both to the leader and to the group. Because of the diversity of individual differences inherent in any group, conflict and controversy are potentially present.

Yet, some conference leaders either fail to recognize this hidden force or they ignore it altogether. In such cases, conferences may become nothing more than sessions of "billing and cooing" or of uncontrolled controversy.

The successful conference leader recognizes that personal freedom is important to creativity. However, leaders may limit the creative freedom of conferees by failing to deal with the negative aspects—such as conformity, passivity, mediocrity, or manipulation—of group thinking.

For example, the response of the leader or conferee to the suggestion of another participant may be, "But that's not the way we've been doing it," or "We always promote this activity in March." The fact that the project has never quite succeeded in March seemingly has made little impact on some of the participants. For them the die is cast. They are slaves to conformity.

How can the leader unshackle a group from these slavish conference habits? How can he stimulate and control a healthy exchange of ideas? The following suggestions may be helpful:

1. Develop a democratic or cooperative leadership. The democratic leader has a liberating effect on others, while the auto-

cratic leader stifles and limits discussion. The democratic leader is interested in the creative freedom of conferees, in member interaction, in reaching the best group decisions, and in having participants satisfy their personal needs.

In such an atmosphere, discussion and interaction take place freely. In this environment, leadership is shared. The various abilities inherent in a group suggest the possibility that it can reach quality decisions and arrive at better solutions than an individual is able to do alone.

2. Maintain group interaction until the participants are ready for a group decision. Accept contributions, facts, comments, ideas, or questions from any conferee. Let each individual discuss his solution to the problem. A conference group in which the members identify with one another is usually one in which interpersonal relations are conducive to quality problem-solving.

Encourage those with adverse ideas to speak out. Everyone needs to understand the thinking of each person. When conflicting ideas produce sharp controversy, the leader steps in to restate each person's opinion in a way that is satisfactory to those involved. Usually, this action clarifies arguments and produces understanding.

A group without differences of opinion and conflict may be in serious trouble. When points of view are withheld, the best solution may never be reached.

The leader, as well as the conferees, must understand that a participant's differing opinion is not necessarily personal. When this fact is understood, the problem can be dealt with by the group, free from emotional involvement. Personality conflicts are often difficult to resolve. Generally, the meeting ends in an impasse. The leader, then, must develop habits and skills in his conference behavior (speaking and listening) which encourage conferees to express freely their differing points of view.

Sometimes conflict and controversy result from deficiencies in language and communication skills, particularly in the inability of some conferees to interpret and weigh facts and figures properly. Group permissiveness dwindles when members react subjectively to factual data and arrive at pseudosolutions by way of hunches.

One of the greatest deterrents to good group action is that some people feel a necessity to suppress their real opinions in the interest of group harmony. Pseudoagreement results. The best, but unheard, arguments may walk out of the conference room when the meeting adjourns.

Conference leaders must learn that people will interact only when leaders respect, cherish, and recognize individual differences rather than suffocate them. Out of a climate of permissiveness and mutual appreciation, leaders can stimulate people to contribute ideas and to reach quality decisions.

• Summarize the discussion. Throughout the course of the meeting, the leader briefly reviews from time to time what has gone on before in order to bring everyone up to date. He secures a concensus and states conclusions reached and/or actions recommended.

• Make assignments, if necessary. Usually, group decisions require some sort of follow up action. The leader is responsible for making definite assignments to one or more workers to carry out the recommended actions. In most cases, the workers would apply the solutions to their own jobs.

• Adjourn the group at the agreed upon time. Any exception should have the approval of the group.

• Evaluate the results of the meeting after adjournment. The leader should measure his own effectiveness as a conference leader. Some questions he may ask himself are:

> Did I present the problem clearly?
> Did I refer their questions to the group instead of trying to take over and answer them myself?
> Did I talk too much?
> Did I pull into the discussion the person, or persons, who said little or nothing?
> Did I stimulate their thinking?
> Did I give conferees time to think?
> Did I summarize clearly the thinking of the group?
> Did I control distractions?

Did I give everyone an opportunity to express himself?
Did the meeting fulfil its purpose?

What Follow-up Is Necessary?

The real value of any meeting may not be realized until days, weeks, or even months later when the decisions reached in one or more meetings are applied to the problems, projects, program actions, or activities.

For this reason, following through on decisions agreed upon is very important. Generally, "follow through" is the most neglected area of the entire conference process. To avoid this omission, set up a program that checks, examines, prods, and guides those charged with responsibility to apply agreed-upon solutions to their work assignments.

Let it not be said of your staff meetings, "We discuss everything but never seem to settle or accomplish anything."

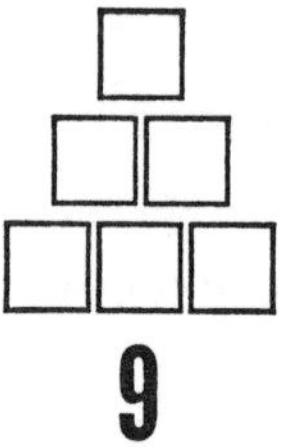

9

The Role of the Personnel Committee

The personnel committee in a church is a connecting link between the paid staff and the church in matters related to personnel administration and management.

It acts mainly as a policy-making group. It usually initiates and gets church approval of policies and procedures in areas such as staff organization, employment practices, salaries, benefits, and personnel services.

It may assist, when called upon, in relieving the pastor of minor administrative details. The members of the personnel committee do not usurp the supervisory and administrative responsibilities of the pastor or any staff person.

The pastor attends, and has a vital part in, all the meetings and deliberations of the personnel committee. Furthermore, it is his responsibility to explain the approved personnel policies and procedures to the paid staff workers and to get their acceptance.

Since the undergirding principles of Christian devotion and understanding should always be foremost in the personnel committee's ministry, it is extremely important that the church choose wisely the members to serve on this committee. Although some phases of the committee's work may seem to be technical, they can be performed well by men and women who have good judgment, are objective, and have demonstrated the ability to work well with others.

The following suggestions for the personnel committee may be applied to a church staff of any size.

Establish Employment Practices

This responsibility includes setting up employment qualifications and skills. It also may include giving assistance to the pastor, when requested, in recruiting, interviewing, and placing the new worker on the job. The chairman of the personnel committee may take part or all of the steps leading to the employment of a worker. Or he may assign the task to another member of the committee.

In a large church the minister of education, business administrator, or other staff supervisor usually recruits, interviews, and places on the job those workers for whom he has supervisory responsibility. Especially does this procedure apply when filling a clerical or manual vacancy.

Usually, when a church approves the addition or replacement of a professional staff worker such as minister of education, minister of music, the full personnel committee acts to assist the pastor in finding, interviewing, and recommending a qualified person for church approval.

Whatever employment procedure is used, it is desirable for the person on the church staff who is to supervise the new employee to be given an opportunity to interview the applicant and to share in the employment decision.

The personnel committee should formulate written employment policies and procedures that will serve as a guide to the staff. See chapter 1 for a more detailed review of suggested employment practices.

- Daily and weekly work-hour schedules.

The pastor and the personnel committee should decide and establish the number of work hours for each day (seven, seven and one-half, eight, or more); the work-day schedule (8:00 to

5:00, 8:30 to 5:30, or other); and the work-week schedule (five days, five and one-half days, or other).

• Salary program.

The personnel committee is the logical one to initiate and set up a formalized salary plan for church approval. The salary program includes office and manual workers and may also include professional staff workers such as pastor, minister of education. See chapter 5 for suggestions in establishing a salary plan.

The writing of a description for each position on the paid staff—part-time or regular—is a requisite to establishing a salary plan. See chapter 4 for suggestions in writing job descriptions.

• Employee services.

The work of the personnel committee may include assistance to employees in areas such as providing weekday parking space, locating a room, apartment, or house for new workers, arranging for medical service in the event an employee becomes ill or is injured while at work, or arranging credit at a local source.

• Future personnel expansion.

As a church grows, additional staff workers will be needed from time to time. It is the responsibility of the personnel committee to make periodic studies of the work load of the church staff to determine any necessary expansion needs.

The pastor may initiate the request for an additional worker. It is the duty of the personnel committee to review the request with him or with other supervisory staff members, then, if in order, to request church approval for action.

The addition of an office employee may require a restudy of one or more clerical job descriptions and a reassignment of some of the various job duties before a new description and job title are determined and before a new worker is employed. See chapter 4.

The personnel committee, prior to bringing its recommendation to the church, may need to work with the budget or finance committee to determine if additional salary funds are available in this year's budget.

• Review of staff organization chart.

Periodically, review the organizational relationship of the paid staff workers to one another. An organization chart shows these relationships. As a church staff increases in number, organization relationship patterns usually require review and modification. See chapter 3.

The organization chart should be updated every time a new worker is added to the staff.

Provide Employee Benefits

Most churches provide employee benefits, some churches more than others. Sometimes a pastor and the personnel committee learn of the need to review and upgrade the church's employee benefits when they interview a prospective professional worker. The tendency is to offer the prospective worker benefits to match those of his present position. If they exceed those of present staff members, sooner or later problems will arise. It is important for every employee to be treated fairly in the matter of employee benefits.

Most pastors desire adequate benefits for staff workers. However, one could find himself in an awkward position trying to initiate proposals if he is directly involved. Then, certainly, the need of a personnel committee is apparent. It is the logical committee to study, draft, and implement a reasonable and appropriate plan of benefits for church staff members. Such a plan should include every person paid by the church for his services. Regular part-time workers should be considered also. Exceptions might be those employees classified as temporary and those who work less than half time.

The question as to what constitutes a good plan of employee benefits often arises. Practice varies from one church to another just as the benefit plans of business establishments vary.

The personnel committee, however, should give consideration to a group of standard benefits generally included for workers. Such a group includes vacations, holidays, hospitalization, life insurance, retirement pension, sick leave, Christmas gift, paid moving expenses, housing allowance, car expense, and others. The personnel committee may wish also to consider benefits related to outside invitations, such as revivals and educational meetings, received by staff members.

As the personnel committee surveys the field of possible benefits and decides which ones to include or upgrade, it also should consider whether newly included benefits will be contributory or noncontributory. A contributory benefit requires that staff members pay part of the cost. Examples might be hospitalization, life insurance, and retirement. When staff members are asked to pay part of the cost of a new benefit, their approval should be obtained before the benefit is adopted. After that, when new workers are added to the staff they would automatically enter the plan.

The following suggestions are steps that the personnel committee may follow in initiating a plan of benefits or in upgrading the present plan:

• Survey the benefits presently provided for staff workers by the church. The church may not have in written form statements outlining the various benefits. Or such statements may be recorded here and there in church minutes that cover several years of church action.

Seek the guidance and counsel of the pastor and other staff workers in gathering the information. Inquire as to the staff workers' interpretation of present benefits. Check the salary records to learn which paid staff members, if any, are included in a contributory or noncontributory benefit. List their names.

Prepare a graph of the findings. List the names of all staff members, including regular part-time workers on the left-hand side of the page. Across the top write in all the benefits which the church presently provides, even if some do not apply to every staff worker. Draw lines across and down the page dividing names and benefits. Place a check in the squares thus formed across the page by each name to identify benefit participation. The graph is your work sheet. See Exhibit XIX.

- Make a survey of the benefits offered by other churches to their staff workers. Such information is especially valuable if the members of the personnel committee do not have too much information or experience in setting up a benefit plan. It is entirely possible that the results of this survey may reveal a general low level and static benefit condition. If so, the committee may wish to talk to various business men in the church to learn what benefits they receive or offer to their employees. After all, churches should try to maintain a competitive position in order to attract top notch office and manual workers.
- Decide on the new benefits to be included and the present benefits to be upgraded. Study each benefit separately and carefully. Seek the advice and counsel of the pastor and ask for his considered judgment in final determinations.

The vacation policy, for example, may not be adequate. Perhaps one week of vacation is allowed after one year of service. The personnel committee may wish to increase the vacation time benefit for an employee to two weeks after one year of service, to three weeks for a person with ten (or fifteen) years of service, and to four weeks for a person with twenty (or twenty-five) years of service. Also the personnel committee may desire to expand the benefit to include all staff members—custodians, maids, office workers, and others not presently covered.

Six or seven holidays a year are usually included for workers in business establishments. A church should provide similar holiday benefits. The standard holidays are New Year's Day, Independence Day, Labor Day, Thanksgiving Day, and Christmas. Usually a day or a half day is given as Christmas Eve holiday. Other holidays which have local or state significance are sometimes included.

An important item which the personnel committee may wish to consider is group insurance that includes medical and life insurance. Local insurance companies will be glad to explain various plans and their cost.

EXHIBIT XIX

CHART SHOWING EMPLOYEE BENEFIT PARTICIPATION

	Pension Plan		Social Security		Medical Plan		Life Insurance		Vacation	Holidays	Sick Leave with Pay	Housing Allowance	Christmas Gift	Revivals and Educational Mtgs	Parking Space	Rest Periods	(other)	(other)
NAME	C	NC	C	NC	C	NC	C	NC										
TOTALS																		

C – Employee contributes
NC – Employee does not contribute; church pays all

Another important benefit is retirement pension. Most churches include the pastor, minister of education, minister of music, business administrator, and other professional staff workers in a pension plan. The personnel committee may well consider bringing all regular staff members under the same pension plan. This would be in addition to Social Security.

A church which has no pension plan or does not include all its regular workers may find it necessary, at each worker's retirement time, to make one of several subjective decisions: to do nothing; to do something; or, to be generous. The decision usually depends upon how much direct monthly expense the church at the time is able to afford. The better plan, of course, is for the church to budget pension costs annually over the work life of each employee.

Other benefits such as sick leave, parking, housing allowance, car expense, should be given similar exploratory treatment.

• Prepare a clear and complete statement of each item to be included in the overall benefit plan. The members of the personnel committee and the pastor, must agree in their understanding and interpretation of each item in the proposed total benefit plan. The best way to reach understanding is for the chairman of the personnel committee to prepare carefully written statements of each benefit, including limitations, conditions of coverage, and of the staff members to whom each shall apply. Benefits should be written in the form of church policy. See Exhibit XX for a suggested policy format.

• Prepare an analysis of the cost of each benefit. When new benefits are included or present benefits upgraded, the cost to the church is usually increased. After careful study, the committee may find that the cost of desired increased benefits cannot be budgeted until the following year. Or a longer range program covering two or more years may be considered in establishing the overall revised benefit plan. The personnel committee may find that some of the increased benefits such as vacation, holidays, or sick leave may be implemented immediately.

The course taken depends upon the cost involved. The cost is

EXHIBIT XX

POLICY

(Suggested Format)

SUBJECT: Vacation policy (example only)

PURPOSE: To establish policy concerning vacations for regular employees

POLICY:

1. One week is granted after six months of continuous service and a second week after completing twelve months of continuous service. Both weeks may be taken as a unit after completing twelve months of continuous service.
2. Employees who have completed ten years of service are eligible for three weeks of vacation.
3. Employees who have completed twenty years of service are eligible for four weeks of vacation.
4. The pastor shall be entitled to four weeks of vacation each year.
5. The pastor and other staff supervisors shall by January 1 arrange vacation schedules so that time off will not seriously handicap the work or require employment of temporary workers except in extreme emergencies.
6. The vacation is considered as being applicable to and for the calendar year.
7. An employee may have an additional week of vacation without pay upon the pastor's approval.

POLICY (continued)

8. Paid holidays which occur during the employee's vacation are to be added to the beginning or end of the vacation period.
9. Vacation periods may be divided but not less than units of one week.
10. Vacation time is not accumulative from one year to the next; nor can an employee use vacation time in a current year that would be earned in the following year.
11. Employees will not receive additional pay for a vacation not taken.
12. When at least two weeks' notice of termination is given, the employee will receive vacation allowance pay for onehalf of unused vacation if termination occurs before July 1 and full allowance pay if termination occurs July 1 or later.
13. Any deviation from this policy must be approved by the most immediate supervisor and the pastor.

recurring year after year, and it increases as new workers are added to the staff. Also the church which presently has very few benefits may not wish to "cram its program full" the first year, even if it could afford the cost.

The personnel committee should consult with the budget committee or other church committee charged with the responsibility for reviewing new cost programs.

• Present the proposed benefit plan to the church for approval and adoption. Prepare copies for distribution at the time the proposed plan is read, explained, and recommended to the church for approval. Perhaps a summary statement of the findings of comparable benefit programs in other churches or business establishments may be helpful and informative. Be ready to give increased cost figures. With the cooperation of the budget or finance chairman, show how the increased costs can presently be absorbed, or what additional budget requirements, if any, are necessary.

• After church approval and with the assistance of the pastor, explain details of the benefit program to the paid church workers.

• Assign responsibility for the continued implementation and interpretation of benefit policies. Members of the personnel committee are not always available to discuss the benefits with new workers or to review or to interpret them to those who have served on the staff for several years. The most practical solution is for the pastor to assume this assignment as one of his administrative responsibilities. He, in turn, shares this responsibility with staff supervisors.

Copies of the benefit policies should be kept in an assigned office along with the personnel records.

• Review the benefits periodically. Perhaps every three to five years the entire benefit plan should be reviewed by the personnel committee.

Employee benefits are an accepted part of present-day economy. Salaries and benefits go together. They make up the compensation package. The benefits which a church provides its staff members are extremely important to the worker on the job as well as to the prospective worker as he considers joining the staff.

Most church members desire a good benefit program for their staff members. They usually will approve one if the matter is brought to their attention in a well-organized presentation. The personnel committee renders a significant service when it studies, drafts, recommends, and implements a reasonable and acceptable church employee benefit plan.

Prepare a Personnel Policies and Procedures Manual

A policy is a guiding principle on which to base future action. A procedure is an organized grouping of statements related to a certain action that answers the questions who, what, when, and how.

The personnel policies and procedures manual usually includes a church staff organization chart (see chapter 3), a set of position descriptions of all the paid staff workers (see chapter 4), salary scales (see chapter 5), in addition to a set of policies and procedures covering absences, employee benefits, employment practices, leaves of absence, salary administration and miscellaneous items. See Exhibits XX and XXI for sample policy and procedure formats.

A partial listing of items which the pastor and the personnel committee may wish to review for possible inclusion in a policies and procedures manual is as follows:

- Absence

Death in the immediate family of a worker. (One, two or more days time off? or give time off without stating days? time off with pay?)

Attendance at funerals of more distant relatives or friends, or to serve as pallbearer. (How much time off? one or two hours or a half day? or give time off without stating hours?)

Hospitalization and convalesence. (How much time off with pay? four, eight, twelve, or more weeks? indefinitely?)

Jury duty. (Will the worker receive full pay in addition to his jury fees? or salary minus jury fees?)

Medical appointments during work hours. (How much time

EXHIBIT XXI

PROCEDURE

(Suggested Format)

SUBJECT: Weekly Bulletin--Publishing the (Example only)

PURPOSE: To guide employees in publishing the bulletin

PROCEDURE:

Professional workers

1. Prepare copy and place on desk of pastor's secretary by 1:00 each Monday afternoon.

Pastor's Secretary (or other)

2. Edit copy; type according to printing specifications; mark type and prepare layout.
3. Work with professional staff to enlarge, change, or cut copy to fit space.
4. Place completed copy and layout on pastor's desk by 8:00 A.M. Tuesday.

Pastor

5. Check copy and layout; upon approval return to secretary's desk by noon Tuesday.

Pastor's Secretary

6. Deliver copy to printer by 1:00 P.M. Tuesday for Thursday noon delivery.
7. Distribute one copy to each staff member and file five copies.
8. Deliver remaining copies to clerk-typist's desk by 2:00 P.M. Thursday.

Clerk-typist

9. Operate the addressing machine; stuff, seal, stamp, and tie the envelopes for mailing.

10. Give to church custodian by 4:30 P.M. Thursday for delivery to the post office.

Custodian

11. Deliver bulletins to post office before 5:00 P.M. Thursday.

without payroll deduction? one, two, or more hours on each occasion?)

Personal illness. (Time off with pay, or by some other plan?)

Personal reasons. (Time off with or without pay?)

Voting time. (Time off during the work day? Polls are usually open from seven to seven).

- Employee benefits

Accident insurance. (Cover all the employees? a few? none?)

Advance salary. (Will the church permit an employee to request his salary check before payday? If so, under what circumstances?)

Benefit status during leave of absence. (Will the church continue a worker on all benefits, some of them, or none? If some or all benefits are continued, up to how many months? If some of the benefits are contributory, will the employee on leave of absence be expected to pay his portion?)

Benefit status during military leave. (Will the benefits be continued or frozen? Usually, the insurance benefits are terminated, the pension plan frozen, and time spent in military service counted as continued church job tenure for purposes of figuring vacation eligibility and service awards).

Car expense. (For whom on the staff and how much?)

Employee training program. (Will the church encourage its paid workers to enrol in correspondence courses; night or day courses in a local school or college? If so, how much cost assistance, if any? Or will there be cost assistance if the employee takes courses at night and Saturday only?)

Group insurance—hospitalization and life. (Will the church pay all costs or employee pay part? Will all regular workers be included in the plan?)

Holidays. (Five, six, seven, or more? which holidays? When will a holiday be taken if it falls on a Saturday or a Sunday?)

Housing allowance. (How much, if any? and for whom?)

Marriage of an employee. (How much time off with pay for the honeymoon? two, three, or more days?)

Moving expenses. (For all new employees who join the staff?

Will the church or the worker arrange for the carrier? Will the employee pay all costs and be reimbursed by the church? Or will the new worker submit the bill to the church for payment?)

Pension plan. (Are all employees covered? Will the church pay all costs or employees share in the cost? Or will the church pay all costs of some employees and part cost of the others?)

Physical examinations. (Should the church provide annual physical examinations for any of its workers? If so, for whom and how much cost assistance?)

Pulpit supply. (How many Sundays each year will the church be responsible for giving an honorarium to a supply preacher? How much?)

Rest periods. (One or two rest periods each work day? How much time? ten, fifteen, twenty minutes, or more, for each rest period?)

Revivals and education meetings. (How many weeks away each year? Would this benefit be extended to others as well as the pastor? If so, to whom?)

Service recognition awards. (How often? each five, ten, fifteen, twenty, years of service? Type of recognition? gift, money, or other?)

Social Security. (The local Social Security office has information outlining benefits).

Travel insurance. (For all, part, or none of the staff? How much coverage, if any? Who pays cost?)

Vacation. (What tenure is required to be eligible for one week, two weeks, three, or more, of vacation? Are all regular workers included in the plan? Will some workers have a different schedule of vacation time allowed? Must vacations be taken in units of a week or more or can an employee take a day or two at a time? Can vacations be carried over from one year to the next? Who schedules vacations of the workers?

- Employment practices

Employment of husband and wife. (Is employment on the staff of two members of the same household acceptable?)

Employment of relatives. (Any exception? If so, what?)

Expansion of personnel. (Who initiates the request? Who approves?)

Forced termination. (For what reasons should a person be dismissed? What steps, if any, should guide the supervisor in dismissing a worker?)

Personal qualifications. (What qualifications are required for consideration for employment? age? education? experience? physical requirements? church membership?)

Reemployment of military personnel. (Refer to legal requirements).

Reemployment of retirees. (Should you consider reemployment of church retired workers? If so, on what basis?)

Regular part-time employment. (What benefits will these employees receive, if any? On what basis will their hourly rate be figured?)

Resignation notice. (Should the church require one week's notice, two, or more, from an employee who plans to terminate? What penalty, if any, such as loss of vacation allowance, should be imposed when the employee does not give the required notice? Should any exceptions to a penalty be written into a policy?)

Screening applicants. (What requirements? use of application form? interviewing? testing? obtaining character and business references? others?)

Temporary employment. (When shall temporary employees be used? What is the length of time a temporary worker can be kept on the payroll? What is the basis for determining the hourly rate?)

Vacation allowance pay. (When an employee terminates, how much of his unused vacation, if any, should be paid him?)

- Leave of absence

College or seminary study leave. (Who, if anyone, will be eligible for a quarter, semester, or more, of study? Upon what basis will eligibility be determined? tenure of service or other? Will the leave be with or without pay? If without pay, will benefits be continued?)

Military service. (Refer to the legal requirements).

Maternity. (Grant a leave of absence or terminate the worker? If a leave is granted, for how long?)

Temporary disability. (With or without pay? If with pay, for how many months? Will benefits be continued during the interim period?

- Salary administration

Demotion of a worker. (For what reasons? Is salary adjustment involved? if so, what?)

Dismissal pay. (How much pay, if any, beyond last work day? one week? two weeks? or more? Should the dismissal paycheck include unused vacation time?)

Payroll deductions. (What items will be deducted from salary checks?)

Promotion to a higher job. (On what basis will the salary be determined? promotability? How processed?)

Salary increases. (On what basis will salaries of employees be increased? automatic? every January? based on tenure of service? based on job performance? Can an employee's salary be increased more than one step at a time?)

- Miscellaneous

Garnishments. (What action, if any, will the church take in the matter of employee garnishments?)

Membership in professional, civic, and service organizations. (Will the church pay all, part, or none of the cost? If all or part of the cost is paid by the church, who on the staff is eligible to participate?)

Parking. (Will special places be assigned to all or only to part of the paid staff workers during the work week? on Sunday?)

Personnel records. (What records, if any, will be set up? application file? individual salary records? pension and group insurance records? Who will maintain the records?)

Work day schedule. (How many hours a day? What are the starting and closing times?)

Work week schedule. (How many days a week? five? five and one-half days or more? staggered schedule on Saturday?)

Formalized personnel policies and procedures, which are carefully considered and tailored to fit the needs of a church, almost eliminate the necessity for making decisions each time an emergency situation arises. In making these provisions, the personnel committee frees the pastor and his staff to perform their tasks more effectively and efficiently.